Past Life Regression

A GUIDE FOR PRACTITIONERS

Past Life Regression

A GUIDE FOR PRACTITIONERS

Mary Lee LaBay

© Copyright 2004 Mary Lee LaBay.
All rights reserved. No part of this publication may be reproduced, stored in a retrieval system, or transmitted, in any form or by any means, electronic, mechanical, photocopying, recording, or otherwise, without the written prior permission of the author.

Cover design – Lee Ater
Book layout – James LaBay
Editor – Ceci Miller

Note for Librarians: a cataloguing record for this book that includes Dewey Decimal Classification and US Library of Congress numbers is available from the Library and Archives of Canada. The complete cataloguing record can be obtained from their online database at: www.collectionscanada.ca/amicus/index-e.html
ISBN 1-4120-1278-3

TRAFFORD

Offices in Canada, USA, Ireland, UK and Spain
This book was published on-demand in cooperation with Trafford Publishing. On-demand publishing is a unique process and service of making a book available for retail sale to the public taking advantage of on-demand manufacturing and Internet marketing. On-demand publishing includes promotions, retail sales, manufacturing, order fulfilment, accounting and collecting royalties on behalf of the author.

Book sales for North America and international:
Trafford Publishing, 6E–2333 Government St.,
Victoria, BC v8t 4p4 CANADA
phone 250 383 6864 (toll-free 1 888 232 4444)
fax 250 383 6804; email to orders@trafford.com

Books sales in Europe:
Trafford Publishing (UK) Ltd., Enterprise House, Wistaston Road Business Centre, Wistaston Road, Crewe, Cheshire CW2 7RP UNITED KINGDOM
phone 01270 251 396 (local rate 0845 230 9601)
facsimile 01270 254 983; orders.uk@trafford.com

Order online at:
www.trafford.com/robots/03-1656.html

10 9 8 7 6 5 4

In loving memory of my dad,
Maurice Lee LaBay 1921-2002

Acknowledgments

It has taken nearly 20 years of research and experience to acquire the information, knowledge, and stories that have become a part of this book. It will be difficult to give full credit to all the participants who have contributed. However, many people have had a direct impact on this work, and it is with deep gratitude and pleasure that I acknowledge them here.

Heartfelt gratitude to my best friend, Lee Ater, for the artistic design of all my printed materials, including the cover of this book. Thank you for being such a loyal and encouraging friend.

Loving appreciation also to my brother, James LaBay, not only for the artistically pleasing design of the interior of the book, but also for his lifelong love and friendship. This life is just one of the many we have shared. I love and admire you so much.

Special appreciation to my editor, Ceci Miller, whose assistance and contributions to this work have been invaluable in helping to bring my vision for this project into a finished form.

Loving gratitude to Scott Wetstone, my life partner. Thank you for giving me the space, time, support, and environment to concentrate on this work. You have allowed me to bring the dream of this book into reality. Thank you, my love!

I wish also to acknowledge all my friends who supported this effort, read copies of the manuscript, gave their opinions, and stood by me throughout the whole process. In particular, I want to thank Marcie Draheim, Jann Finley-Epps, Sue Tribolini, and Hank Wesselman. Your comments, suggestions, and encouragement have been greatly appreciated.

I value the opportunities, encouragement, and assistance I have received from Trafford Publishing.

Special acknowledgment and gratitude to my clients and fellow students who, over the years and through every regression, have brought me your memories, experiences, and perceptions, contributing to my understanding and skills. Many of your memories are included in this work, and I am grateful that you agreed to share your stories with the world. Through our work together, we have each had the opportunity to grow, while making a contribution to the collective knowledge about past life regression.

My love and gratitude encircle my mother, Margery LaBay, and my children, Quincy and London Miller. Your loving energy warms my heart. To Dad: Thank you for your support throughout our time together during this earth walk. You taught me so much on many levels. Your experiences at the end of your life, and beyond, contributed richly to my knowledge of this subject.

Contents

Introduction 11

ONE
Why Explore Past Lives in Counseling? 15
    Cycles of Behavior 16
    Physical Healing 17
    Unexplained Pain 22
    Phobias 23
    Life Purpose 24
    Clarifying Core Values 28
    Recognizing People We Have Known Before 29
    Marriage and Divorce 34
    Childhood Abuse 35
    Parenting and Adoption 38
    Soul Groups 39

TWO
Why We Forget 41
    Life's Distractions 41
    Societal Norms 42
    Avoidance 42
    Reframing: Opening the Door to Self-Acceptance 46

THREE
How We Remember 47
    Techniques for Past Life Regression 47
    Script for Past Life Regression 49
    Other Factors in Past Life Regression 50
    The Scientific Method and Beyond 52
    Imagination 53
    Strategies to Expand and Exercise the Imagination 53
    Belief 54

FOUR
False Memory, Real Memory, and Filters 57
Matching Memories 59
Sorting Out Memory from Fantasy 60
Filtering Reality 62
Modes of Experience: Visual, Auditory and Kinesthetic 64
So What Is Real? 66

FIVE
Special Considerations 69
Remembering the Death Experience 69
Grieving 71
Reconnecting with Life Purpose 75
Which Lifetime to Experience? 78
Visiting the Future 78
How Many Lifetimes? 80
Other Worlds, Other Possibilities 80
Old Soul or New Soul? 81
Dimensions and Awareness 82
Astral Plane 83
Concepts of Time 84
Point of Focus 84
True Success 86
Was Everyone Famous? 86
Can You Be Your Own Ancestor? 90

SIX
Stepping In and Stepping Out 91
Mutual Agreements Between Souls 92
What Happens to the One Who Leaves? 93
Why Step Out? 94
Why Step In? 95
Who Keeps the Personality? 95

    An Uncommon Experience 96
    Stepping In Versus Possession 97

SEVEN
Life Between Lives **99**
    Perception Alters Experience.. 100
    So What Does Happen? 101
    Pre-Birth Choices and Experience 104
    Making Decisions.. 106
    A Personal Experience 109

EIGHT
Techniques for Healing During Regression **113**
    Removing Blocks 113
    Object Imagery and Metaphor 116
    Secondary Gains, Parts Therapy and Their Outcomes 119
    Removing the Analytical Imp 124
    Soul Retrieval 126
    Carrying Wisdom from One Life to the Next 127

NINE
Integrating the Work **129**
    Homework for the Client 132

Epilogue **137**

Introduction

As counselors, coaches, body workers, healers, and therapists, we are constantly seeking new or alternative ways to assist our clients in their journey toward healing and self-discovery. Myriad tools and techniques are available, and new ones regularly emerge. Although the concept of reincarnation and the exploration of past lives have persisted throughout history, the use of past life regression as a therapy and personal growth tool has gained significant popularity since the latter part of the twentieth century. Once a mysterious subject rarely accessible to the public, past life regression appears with ever-increasing frequency in movies, on talk shows, in magazines and books, and, quite notably, in the therapy office. The techniques of past life regression can effectively support any complementary health practice, and also provide your client with valuable insights for self-awareness and healing.

This text is designed to introduce you to the multi-faceted world of past life regression. You may wish to apply this knowledge for your own personal discovery; however, here you will be learning primarily how to incorporate these skills into your counseling practice—to assist your clients in more deeply exploring who they are, and to help them expand their perception of the world. The material contained here will give you all the necessary skills and techniques to conduct safe and successful past life regressions. Excerpts from client sessions are included here by permission, to illustrate the wide variety of benefits available to clients through past life regression technique. Whether you are learning these skills for the first time, or adding to what you already know of the subject, I trust that this material will be a valuable resource for you.

If this is your first acquaintance with past life regression, it is likely that your perceptions—of the world, your life experiences, and your clients—will be forever altered by the material presented here.

Past life regression is a topic close to my heart. For this reason I have given the subject years of study, research, and personal exploration. I have always felt that each of us has lived before. I knew it as a child; I assumed it as an adult. There was never a doubt in my mind. When I began to experience my own past life regressions, I was excited to finally have personal knowledge of this dimension of life. These experiences continually lead me to a greater understanding of myself—my character strengths and weaknesses, my patterns of behavior, my purpose, and, more importantly, where I am going from here. Opening the portal to my past lives inspired me to remain steadfast on my spiritual journey of self-discovery, healing, and greater wholeness.

The knowledge available concerning reincarnation and past life regression has changed and developed throughout the years. Although this work is at the leading edge of the subject to date, it is expected—and desirable—that the information contained herein will be superseded in the coming years as the knowledge and understanding of the universe we live in continues to advance.

In these pages I have endeavored to pass along the knowledge and skills I have acquired over the years, so that the results of this work can be attained by many more people than I can personally reach. By experiencing and facilitating past life regressions, I have witnessed fascinating memories and marvelous results—and you can, too!

Past Life Regression

A GUIDE FOR PRACTITIONERS

CHAPTER ONE
Why Explore Past Lives in Counseling

Past life regression is the deliberate use of a variety of methods to retrieve memories of experiences that occurred in other lifetimes. While re-experiencing past life events often brings about healing and change, the goal of looking beyond the veil of separation into the memories of the subconscious mind is to gather knowledge, wisdom, and understanding of the deeper aspects of personality and character. The larger objective is the pursuit of completion and wholeness.

In essence, the pursuit of past life memories derives from the desire to put present life experiences, personality, and character into context within the full progression of the soul. To illustrate, imagine that you have amnesia. You cannot remember anything that happened before you were 21 years old. What would you know about yourself?

How could you understand your relationships with other people? What would you know about your personality traits, the origins of your health issues, the basis for your choice of occupation, or the source of your knowledge and wisdom? Without substantiating evidence, it is difficult to truly know yourself.

Expand that example to the bigger picture of the soul. Only by obtaining information about your previous lifetimes can you gain full knowledge of your character, your personality, your purpose, your overall progress, and the nature of your soul.

While clients may come to your office seeking a past life regression simply out of curiosity, the more sophisticated seeker wishes to access this information as a means to a greater end. She wants answers to questions that have arisen in her life, questions that cannot be resolved without access to knowledge that lies outside the boundaries of her present life memories.

Clients unaware of the connection between this present life and past ones may be pleasantly surprised when you introduce this tool as a means to achieve their goals. Past life regression affords clients unique opportunities for greater understanding of patterns of behavior, relationships, health issues, life purpose, talents and interests, and recurring challenges. Past life exploration can expand their perspective of themselves, others, and the world at large.

The excerpted client sessions that follow exemplify a range of presenting problems resolved through past life regression technique.

Cycles of Behavior

Most of us have no trouble seeing strengths and weaknesses in others, but when it comes to seeing our own life situations with clarity, the challenge often seems insurmountable. Viewing the cycles and patterns of behavior recurring throughout many lifetimes, however, grants greater perspective on our unique quirks, habits, struggles, fears, choices, hopes, and dreams.

When our clients view their past lives, a natural distancing occurs. When they see their past life "counterpart" exhibiting the same or similar dysfunctional behaviors or making the same mistakes that they do, they more readily understand the changes they need to make. From this third-party perspective, our clients can allow themselves a more objective assessment of behaviors and decisions.

One of the early regressions I facilitated was with a woman in the Midwest. She described a life on the prairie as an early settler. She saw that in her former lifetime, each day she would wash clothes and hang them on a line to dry, while keeping her attention on the horizon. She was waiting for someone, anyone, to come along and make her life exciting. It was a considerably dull lifetime, so much so that I was starting to feel bad about charging her for the session! During our debriefing, I asked her how she thought that lifetime was significant to her now.

Wide-eyed, she exclaimed that the past life she had recalled was just like her own life now. She realized that she was again fairly isolated, leading a very dull life, and was waiting for someone to knock on her door and change all that. The realization that she achieved that day may have been one that turned her whole world around, reversing lifetimes of unproductive behavior. My client awakened to the fact that if she wanted excitement, she would have to initiate it. She certainly understood that she could not go on repeating the same pattern and expecting a different result. In the previous lifetime, she had died alone and unfulfilled. She was determined to not let that happen again.

Physical Healing

In many cases, the health issues we experience in this life have roots that extend into other lifetimes. For this reason, past life regression can provide information important to healing physical symptoms.

While simply viewing the past life may help your client correct a problem, other techniques may also be employed during the regression to facilitate desired changes. These techniques are fully discussed in my book *Hypnotherapy: A Client-Centered Approach,* and are presented here in an abridged form.

One woman I worked with was very spiritually oriented, studied philosophical topics regularly, and had a curiosity about past lives. She wanted a session in order to meet her spirit guide, learn about her life lessons, and resolve several health issues including a seizure disorder that had begun soon after her marriage. Partly due to the medications she had been taking, she had become depressed and self-destructive. For several years this woman had experienced a grand mal seizure once or twice a year, as well as several milder episodes monthly. She also complained of migraines that felt as though she was "being stabbed in the side of the head with a knife."

The transcript of the session that follows demonstrates the formation of questions to facilitate a regression and illustrates the use of additional techniques (noted in parentheses) described in more detail in Chapter 8. After I have put my client (C) into a trance, the regression begins as she describes the scene:

C: I see grass and sticks. It is daytime and I am alone. I am about 20 years old. Now I see tall trees, a rock, some hills, and a grassy area. I am picking up sticks and putting them into a sling to take them to other people who will use them for fire. I see myself going inside my home. I live with my parents. My mom is home and is preparing food.

ML: Do you know where you are, or the date?

C: I don't know exactly where we are, but the date is 17 AD.

ML: What else do you notice?

C: I am sitting and working with my hands. Now I go outside, up a hill, looking for a man. I'm happy. I sit down and wait. I want him to come with me down the hill. Then I sense there is something dangerous going on. The man doesn't come. Other people are coming, and they want to kill our people. I hide. Many people get hurt. Someone hits me and has his hand on my neck. It's a man, and he shoves my face in the dirt. I'm scared! He hits me with a stick on my back and on my head. It's right where the migraines are. It's pulsating...

ML: If that sensation had a shape and a color, what would it be? (Object Imagery technique)

C: It is reddish pink and looks like a long island.

ML: How could you change it so that you could experience healing and relief?

C: I can change it to white and blue. That feels good.

ML: (After the application of other techniques to prepare the client) I would like you to ask your spirit guide to come and speak with you now. What do you notice about them?

C: There is one guide. He is male, a little older and he's smiling at me. His name is Brian. I ask him what I am supposed to work on, what is my purpose. He shows me someone who fell down, and I'm helping them up. It's a metaphor for my purpose in life, to help people in general, and also to work with a specific person.

ML: Moving on now...to another lifetime that will give you information relevant to you at this time...what do you notice next?

C: I see a wooden door with an old tarnished handle. I'm outdoors, on a large boat. I am a man. I'm standing on the deck, rocking back and forth. It's a calm, mild day. I'm on a merchant ship, making sure that people are doing their jobs. Now I see we are in port. We go to a tavern and are drinking and eating. Everyone else is happy, but I'm nervous, waiting for someone. A couple of big men come in: one sits down with me and the other stands. I think they may be blackmailing me about a deal that I've made. I want to give them what they want so they will leave. I want it to be over with, so I tell them to come to the boat and that I will let them take something off the boat. They are laughing. I feel disgusted. I leave the people there at the tavern and go to the boat. I'm walking around in the hold, thinking about what I did, waiting for the men, daydreaming. They show up and surprise me. I tell them to take what they came for and leave. They pull a gun on me, but I'm not surprised. I suspected that it would end badly. They are laughing and they have a box. I say, "I made a deal with the devil." Then they shoot me. They leave and I sit down next to a crate. I am thinking of what I did, how it was wrong, and how I was trying to take a shortcut. I was smuggling some jewelry in the box.

ML: As I count from three to one, you will know the date and the location of this scene. Three, two, one.

C: It's 1575. I'm an English native, and this occurred in Africa. There are dark people here.

ML: What have you learned from this experience?

C: There are no shortcuts. When working with people, you have to go through the process step by step. I have to be in charge of my own destiny.

ML: Move now to another lifetime. What do you notice next?

C: I'm walking around in a Victorian house. It's my house. I live with my husband and two sons. I'm 35 years old. I am arguing with my husband because I want to have some control in the marriage. It is a happy marriage, otherwise.

ML: What do you know about your husband?

C: He is a banker. I don't work. We are talking about finances; he says "no" to me and won't see my point of view. I'm crying. We go on with life, but I am resentful.

ML: Move ahead in time. What do you notice next?

C: We are older. My son is there with his wife. She and I are talking; I'm telling her that I wanted control of something in my marriage but that it didn't work that way and I have put it behind me. She wants more control also. She is having a baby. I tell her that will be a full-time job.

ML: Moving ahead again until the next relevant event, what do you notice next?

C: I'm old and sick. I can't get out of bed. I am living with my son and daughter-in-law. I enjoy my grandchildren.

ML: Looking back over that lifetime, what were your lessons?

C: I found it hard to conform, but it is important to do so. I was supporting my husband in his career. We had social pressures. I lost a bit of myself in the process.

ML: Do you see any correlations between that lifetime and this one?

C: I am learning to do things for myself now. I am trying to stay in control. Seeing this helps me not to be resentful.

ML: Once again calling in your spirit guide, what do you notice this time?

C: I see an older female this time. I see two guides. Brian is there again. He is male, with a beard and dark eyes. Brian speaks: "You are on the right path." He shows me a scene. There is green grass, a shepherd, and a lamb. The boy is caring for the lamb, which is eating grass. The boy carries the lamb down a hill and gives it water. He also carries a stick that glows with a yellow light. He holds it above his head. It gives him strength and power.

ML: What does this message mean to you?

C: I am the shepherd taking care of children. I'm supposed to take the power. It was mine all along but I didn't realize that. My spirit guide wants me to be more open to his guidance. I need to keep meditating. I should keep learning. Read books, write in my journal. He wants me to wear a gold ring, my wedding ring. I need to get it sized and start wearing it again, for security. He tells me to be happy.

ML: Thanking your guide for his assistance, I would like you to ask him to show you yet another lifetime. What do you see next?

C: There is a curtain with warm red, orange, and brown colors. I'm in a small hut or house. There is a young boy there who is ill. His parents are worried, wringing their hands. I am a man and I am there to heal the boy. I go to him and put my hand on his forehead, calling down a type of energy. I am a conduit to help clear his blocks and give him a jump start. I sense there is something wrong with his stomach and intestines. The energy is working to force some kind of bad stuff out of his feet. I know that he won't die. This involves a lesson for his family: they need to learn to be less concerned with material matters and more concerned with family, the well being of the family as a group. At some level, the boy has decided to be sick so that they will focus on what is really important. He will get well. I can sense his parents' frustration; they can't see past the illness to the deeper problem. I can see that the boy eventually got better, but his parents did not really learn from their experience.

ML: What do you notice next?

C: I leave there and go to the temple. I am a man, maybe 36 or 37 years old. I am single, a priest or holy man with a lot of responsibility for the spiritual well being of people in my area. There are other men who do the same thing. We are in Central or South America, in the jungle, near the west coast of the continent. It is not a coastal town, but it is not far from the coast—maybe a few days' travel by foot. I wear a robe wrapped around me, made of a cotton-like material. I don't have a lot of hair, but what I do have is pulled up.

ML: Moving ahead in time to the next relevant experience, what do you notice next?

C: We are celebrating a high holy day. I am sitting on my chair, or throne, during the ceremony. People from outside the temple bring offerings. They give them to me, or perhaps it is a ceremonial gift to a deity that I represent, I'm not sure. It is the beginning of some season and it is hot. Today there is going to be a lesson in compassion. During the day, someone does something wrong and a young boy is brought before me for punishment. I am to judge what should happen to this boy. Because it is a holiday, I tell the people to be compassionate. We will learn compassion instead of punishment today. The poor people are happy, but the people who have more wealth are upset. They like the rules for the rules' sake. They like to enforce, more than follow, the rules. The celebration continues. I retire to the living chamber where it is less chaotic. I speak with my friend, another priest and teacher who is older than me. He shakes his head and tells me that I like to cause upsets; I like to stir things up. He laughs because he agrees that I was right. He reminds me of my husband's boss in my life now.

ML: What happens next?

C: I am looking out over the river from high above, on a cliff. The river stretches beyond where I can see. I am looking at it and thinking; this is my retreat from my daily work. I am searching my inner self for answers regarding my frustrations with my duties as a leader. What is truly important seems to get bogged down in the daily life of the people who come to us. I need to learn patience. My job is to teach and guide people. I must be patient until they become able to understand these things. I also serve as a role model.

ML: Moving ahead, what do you notice next?

C: I am in an argument with someone. This leads to me take on a student. He is a young boy who is to come into the priesthood. He is my apprentice. In this life, he is my son. I spend a couple of years teaching him. One day there is a solar eclipse. It is daytime, but it is dark. My student and the other people are scared. The priests know that this is a good sign. The eclipse provides energy to be used, energy that we can work with. We have a ceremony. Only the oldest, fully trained priests attend. We are gathered in a circle. We are connected, either by holding hands or by an energy-mind connection. The group focuses on one thought. We make a ritual drawing on the ground that we stand on. The priests are trying to use the energy to raise the vibration or make some molecular patterns of the body move faster. There is a large group focusing this thought and intention at this time. It feels successful. We are pleased with the outcome.

ML: Moving ahead in time, what do you notice next?

C: I am about 47 or 57, at the time of my death. It is time for me to go. My student is there. I'm lying on the bed, talking, and I just die. I feel a sense of satisfaction and accomplishment. I was a teacher. I was successful teaching a lot of people that love is more important than fear. I helped those I was supposed to help.

ML: What correlations do you notice between that lifetime and this one?

C: The lessons are the same. I need to teach love, not fear. I must teach not only the love of humankind but also the love of self, so that people can relate to each other better. I am already doing it. I am helping them to feel better about themselves through my work. I need to take better care of my words so they feel even better inside. My work is to raise the consciousness of others.

Five years after this client began her regressions, she had experienced only one small seizure and no grand mal episodes. Past life regression may not be the only cause of her improvement in health; however, she is happy and leading a relatively normal life.

Another client, a woman diagnosed with multiple sclerosis, came to the office looking for possible past life roots to her health issues. She had experienced a past life regression with another therapist years before that she felt had a positive impact, but she remained unclear as to how that lifetime was relevant to her current situation. We decided to explore the same lifetime once again.

Because she already had a "story line," it was not necessary to spend a lot of time taking the client into a deep trance. I asked her to close her eyes, take a relaxing breath, and tell me what she remembered about that previous regression. In this way, she continued to go deeper and deeper into trance state as she re-experienced the memories.

C: I had a husband who didn't come back from the war. I took that to mean that I wasn't good enough to return to.

ML: Go back to that time, and tell me what you experienced when he left.

C: When he left, I couldn't maintain the house. It was the central home for the community, but it fell into ruin. In later years, life was never the same again. I became a recluse. I couldn't cope. My children had moved on, and I was left alone.

ML: Move toward the end of that lifetime. What do you notice then?

C: I am on the property. I live in a log cabin that is the servants' quarters. It is rough. I'm inside and my daughter is next to me. She is my daughter in this life, too.

ML: What else do you notice about that scene?

C: I am very sad and bewildered, wondering why this has happened to me.

ML: If you could have a conversation with the woman you were in that lifetime, what would you tell her?

C: You didn't do it right. You didn't go on with life. Be happy.

ML: What else do you notice?

C: It fades away. I am in the present, with the music. I see the horizon. The sun is coming up. I see the first light and I am hopeful. This is a new day, even though it hasn't fully emerged.

ML: What have you learned from this?

C: It is all right to let go. I don't have to hold on to the pain. Just because there was disappointment doesn't mean I am not worthy.

ML: Is there anything else you would do for her?

C: I would tell her to go in peace. She did the best she could. She is a loving person, and it is okay to love. She has courage and strength. It is okay to let go and move on. It is time to do it…I still want to understand where the MS comes from.

ML: I would like to ask the subconscious mind to present another image or experience that will help us to understand the cause of the MS and steps to take to heal from it.

C: I see myself outdoors. There is a tent, long and flowing. I go into it. It is the top only. The wind blows around and through it. The tent is just floating in it. It is a bright white light. It is just before this lifetime. I have a big present, wrapped in white paper with gold and blue, with a ribbon. I can move through the gift and also beyond it. It goes into the sky. I am finishing something and releasing it. Now I am above and I am lighter. I didn't have to go and examine it. I can go right through. I'm light. It's lovely.

ML: How does that image correlate to you now, and the MS?

C: I don't need to examine the details of the pain. I can just release and move past it. It's a gift. It reminds me to learn more about myself and to release.

Through this experience, my client was able to understand the past life connections to her emotional state in this life, as well as the ramifications to her physical health. The metaphor of the tent and the gift of light at the end of the regression helped her to understand her attitudes in this lifetime.

In any medical case, be sure to make it clear to your clients that it is important they maintain medications and procedures prescribed by their medical and primary care physicians. Hypnotherapy and past life regression work is not a substitute for traditional medical care.

Unexplained Pain

Unexplained pains and syndromes, chronic pain and illness, birthmarks, and other health-related phenomena frequently have their roots in other lifetimes. The proper use of hypnosis and neurolinguistic programming techniques presented later in this book, and also detailed in my book *Hypnotherapy: A Client-Centered Approach,* can significantly reduce the expression and magnitude of such health challenges during the session.

A female client requested a past life regression to attempt to uncover the basis for unexplained pain in her feet and ankles, and to understand her sense of panic whenever she felt hungry.

By visiting two different lifetimes, she was able to get answers to her questions. In the first life that she recalled, she had been a man. He was going up a set of stairs when he encountered another man, wearing armor, who promptly injured his foot with an ax. Further recollections revealed that her past life counterpart owed the man money and that, although he recovered from the injury, he hobbled on that foot for the rest of his life.

My client revealed that there was a lesson concerning greed in that lifetime, and that her counterpart was unethical and unfair. Through the lessons of those experiences, her soul was encouraged to be generous and to avoid making decisions based on monetary gain.

Continuing with another lifetime, my client discovered that she had been a male slave whose ankles were shackled in punishment for disobedience. In that lifetime, my client learned to be wise in picking the important battles to fight. She noticed strong correlations to this life, where again she has not always invested her energy in the right battles. She realized that she needed to think more carefully before acting or speaking.

We continued to another lifetime, and discovered she had been a boy with a dozen siblings. There was a battlefield nearby, and the boy was cold, wet, hungry, and tired. She discovered that the boy was a prisoner of war and died of hunger in a prison camp. From this revelation, we were able to desensitize her fearful response to hunger in her present life.

Through a series of past life experiences, all revealed during a single session, this client was able to understand more fully the origins and nature of the symptoms she was experiencing. Through the employment of various techniques in the midst of the regression, she was also able to achieve relief from her physical discomfort.

Phobias

A regression can also reveal the roots of a phobia or other emotional block. Sometimes simply having knowledge of the relevant past life experience will be enough to shift the energy, allowing a breakthrough or healing to occur. With the assistance of a qualified facilitator, powerful healing can take place using additional techniques, as indicated in this next session.

A male client wanted to experience a past life regression to uncover clues about his intense phobia of heights. He was unable to enjoy mountain vistas, balconies, or even climbing a ladder. He decided that his condition had become debilitating, and he wanted to put an end to it.

In the session, he regressed to a lifetime during which he was moving across the country in a train of covered wagons, taking his wife and all his possessions. There, he discovered the clues he was seeking. Very few women were on the journey, and three other men in the group became jealous of his relationship with his wife. Together they plotted to get rid of him. One day, the group was traveling past a canyon. Engaging him in a conversation, the three men drew him close to the edge of a cliff. In one swift movement, he was pushed to his death.

In this case, simply viewing that past life was enough to resolve the man's subconscious fears. I heard from him a few months later, and he was delighted to report that he was no longer limited by his previous phobia of heights.

Life Purpose

There are two basic components in any given life: consciousness and existence. Each is dependent on the other, and without these two basic qualities a spirit would not be. Existence provides a location in space/time, and consciousness provides awareness of our existence. Without consciousness we would not be aware of our existence; without existence we would have nothing about which to become conscious.

The continuation of existence and consciousness is the fundamental purpose of every living organism. Everything that we do is based on our ability to survive, both as a human during a lifetime and as a spirit throughout eternity. Our misconceptions about reality and twists within our personal philosophy can produce self-sabotaging behaviors. Throughout one life or many lifetimes, our habits perpetuate these mal-adaptations. Yet, even dysfunctional behaviors are reactions to our basic need for survival—both physically and spiritually. As healing occurs our behaviors and choices become more closely aligned with reality, and our responses more consistently support the continuation of our lives in our bodies and as souls.

By investigating past lives, clients can gain clarity about their life purpose. Contrary to wishful thinking or belief, a spirit is not created with a purpose. The consciousness of that spirit, at its origin, must promptly determine and shape a personal purpose. Without choosing a purpose, that spirit would be extinguished. We see this concept reflected in physical terms when we observe someone without awareness of their purpose or passion, wandering through life and fading away. Their life may come to a physical end, or they may simply continue with barely enough life force operating to keep the body trudging grimly along. For this reason, it is our soul's essential responsibility to explore and recognize our avowed life purpose. This process can certainly be greatly assisted through hypnotherapy techniques and during past life regression.

My clients have also demonstrated secondary purposes. These brief purposes may enhance life lessons and personal growth, and are usually accomplished in a relatively short time. Memories of past lives, therefore, may reveal why we have a natural penchant for music and the arts, or for science or healing. Past lives can explain certain relationships, occupations, hobbies, or interests.

In the following case study, my client was a white male musician and visual artist who wanted to try a past life regression to clarify his connection to the arts. In doing so, he demonstrated that a person can carry out directives from one lifetime to another. This case also shows that we can alternate between races. If we regress often enough to other lives, chances are good that we will discover that each of us has lived as a member of every different race, and that we have lived in a variety of cultures.

My client moved back to a lifetime in the 1940s during which he was a black jazz musician. He had been in a traffic accident in his late 30s. He was badly hurt and had subsequent vision problems. He was able to continue playing music until May 14, 1952, when he was in another car accident and died in a hospital near Chicago. Notice the detail that my client was able to retrieve! Information does not always come through so clearly in a session.

My client proceeded to describe the death experience this way: "I look down at my body. I see the room better than ever. It's so beautiful. There is color everywhere. When I see my body, I see a black man in his 40s, slightly graying and a little overweight. I notice broken limbs and a beat-up body. There are flowers everywhere. But no one is there. I'm floating away. It's okay."

He claimed that his lessons in that lifetime were about expression, tolerance, modesty, and having fun. He had been able to help people through his music.

I asked him to move ahead to the period just prior to his birth, to access information about how he chose his current lifetime. He said that on his deathbed in the previous lifetime he had imprinted the message to "remember what I know." He heard the words "Let it flow. Let it go." He understood that he needed to "do what I could and make it good," to be careful with his body, and always to "find that note." He was to remember to do it his own way, even though he might learn from others.

When I asked my client to assess the intention of the person he was in his previous life, he remarked, "The old man would be happy if he could come back as a white person with great vision. He had a joke. He'd say, 'I think I'm going to be an artist.' He wanted to make paintings because he had never been able to see. He would construct beautiful scenes in his mind. He wanted a vacation or break. He wanted to go to Hawaii or California after this. I'm not supposed to forget him. He had terrible grief around being left behind when he could no longer perform. All the others who had been in the accident were fine, but he never played again. They were going on without him, and he was sad."

It is interesting to note that due to a present life car accident, my client had an injury on the left hand which matched the past life injury. In our session I used additional healing techniques to alter the present life pain in that hand. Afterward my client pursued a career as a professional musician.

When we have reconnected with the talents and skills we accrued in former lifetimes, we can bring the same ability, focus, and knowledge into our present lives. Doing so may generate ideas about new directions for our lives and can give greater confidence in the utilization of our talents.

A female client was a prolific writer of poetry and kept a journal. She wanted a deeper understanding of her passion for these activities and wanted information to help her decide whether to turn her hobby into a livelihood. As the regression begins, she is working as a scribe in a religious setting. She is the only female there. She is directed to sit at a bench and is given a quill pen and a stack of blank paper.

"There is a sense of order. A man with a red robe and a big collar stands at the front of the room. He reminds me of the Hierophant card in the tarot deck. He says, 'Now you can learn.' Another man nods in agreement. I am the only woman, yet I feel accepted by them. There are two other men present who seem to be less important. One of them hands me a scroll. I have the best penmanship, and I am to copy the scroll for masses. I say, 'I'd be happy to.' It feels right that I am there—I love to write.

"I begin writing. I'm very careful; I don't want to make any smudges. I'm not nervous even though they are all watching me. I am thinking that the ledger is so big that my arm will be tired, but I keep writing. They bring me some water. The others move around, talk, and check each other's work. On a shelf to my right are many scrolls and a number of old books. When I take a break to eat, I go straight to these books. I love them. I touch their bindings; they are so beautiful.

"I wrote one of the books; I always notice it on the shelf. There is something about a rose in it. I believe it says *Muses* on the cover. It has a red rose and the binding is black. These are my writings. Now I know that's why I am here...I wrote it...it's a book of poetry."

I ask my client if she can read the name of the author on the cover. She continues: "The author's name is not on the binding. I pull the book off the shelf and look at it. The name is on the lower right, printed in gold. It is well worn: Johanna Smythe. She thinks, 'See, I am different, I spell my name with a *y*.'"

I ask my client what she has learned about her questions concerning her writing in this lifetime. She tells me, "I know that I need to be writing about the feelings of my heart. Sometimes you only have to touch one person to know you've made a difference. When I saw that rose, I knew that I had touched some people. Every blank page is a treasure to me, and I need to write something there."

My client continues to write her poetry and keep her journal, yet now she does so with greater energy and enthusiasm. Now that she understands that her writing is an ancient skill which she mastered lifetimes ago, and that it is part of her soul journey, she feels a new sense of purpose.

Through regression, clients may learn why they have moved away from fulfilling their purposes, avoided committing to their life paths, or strayed from their intended courses.

In the following case, a client came to my office complaining of chronic neck pain. She had been unable to get the pain to subside through any previously attempted methods. She further explained that she wanted to change careers: she longed to move away from her office job and delve into the healing arts. Every time she came close to making that dream a reality, however, she would get very anxious and back away.

To lead her into the past life regression, I asked her to focus on the sensations in her neck using the Object Imagery technique. She described a vision of having a rope around her neck, so I asked her how it came to be there. The vision opened further to reveal that she was being hung on charges of witchcraft. She had been accused of healing people with herbs. I asked her to remove the rope from her neck and heal that area of her body. When she did, I asked her to tell me how her neck felt.

She said that the pain was still there, and added that this time her neck was confined in the stocks. Once again she was being punished and ridiculed for being a witch, after having administered healing herbs to someone. I asked her to step out of the stocks and heal her wounds. Even as she did so, she let me know that she was still feeling pain in her neck.

This time her description revealed that she had been beheaded, once again for practicing witchcraft through her healing arts. I asked her to imagine replacing her head and healing the wound. When she did this, she exclaimed with delight that the pain was completely gone.

Not only did this series of regressions reveal the cause of my client's previously unexplained pain, they also clarified why she felt afraid about pursuing her purpose as a healer. In our follow-up discussions, she confirmed that she had been able to move past her fears and begin to pursue her desire to do healing work, bringing her career goals in line with her life purpose.

~~~

When a person looks at a regal mountain overlooking a sparkling lake and calls it beautiful, it is he who has bestowed purpose and beauty on that scene. Without that conscious observation, nature simply *is*. The same applies to any event, object, or being — it simply is, until someone bestows purpose on it. The bromide, "Everything happens for a purpose," is one way in which people overcome their fear of the chaos that is a natural trait of reality.

Resorting to the saying, "It was meant to be," however, can be fatalistic, and even self-defeating. We sometimes use it to justify our laziness, procrastination, indifference, or negligence. Reality results from a chain of events too complex to have innate meaning. The exception occurs when someone applies thought, energy, action, or some other force in order to alter or manipulate an outcome. If an event was "meant to be," then conscious intention was applied to it before the event occurred. If the event had a purpose, consciousness was applied after the fact. Otherwise, the event is just a fact of reality, a result of natural chaos.

Purpose and meaning do not occur without conscious intervention.

Clarifying Core Values

After experiencing a number of past lives, people typically feel more connected to their greater life plan. My clients also often feel an enhanced responsibility to the planet and its inhabitants, and stronger connection to their personal values.

When clients view their lives not simply from the perspective of their personal issues but in context of the evolution of the planet, human society, and history, their individual hardships become less overwhelming. From the perspective of the communal process, our struggles as individuals have greater meaning. We embrace our part as a participant in the greater flow of universal energy.

A woman came to see me because she wanted to explore past lives in an effort to achieve greater happiness and to enhance her perspective on life. She visited two different lifetimes tied by a common thread. In the first life, my client had been a male potter selling his wares in a marketplace, sometime in early A.D. He was in poor health, made little profit, and lived alone. He died young, yet in that short span it was clear that he had been happy with his life. He had no need to impress anyone. He simply enjoyed his knowledge and skill, and filled a need in society. The potter felt that life was too short to let anything upset his happiness.

Continuing to a second past life, my client viewed a lifetime in which she was a woman receiving treatments for cancer. Again she died relatively young. The lesson displayed was to make the most of every day, as you don't know how long you will live. The message was not to wait for happiness, not to think of it as something that will happen in the future. In response to witnessing these past life regressions, my client vowed to stop her negative thoughts and to let go of the day's small irritations.

Recognizing People

People carry a similar energy pattern, or aura, from life to life. The pattern may change as they master lessons or experience traumatic events, yet the distinct nature of that person's energy, even when it appears in a different body, allows one to recognize a former alliance when it reappears.

People often take on similar physical attributes from life to life, such as body type and coloring, behavior and demeanor. One may also use one's own energetic sense to feel and recognize another's energy.

Ask your client to search for recognition by looking into the eyes of someone he is viewing during a past life regression. There is truth in the statement that the eyes are the windows of the soul. Keep in mind that a person may incarnate into any race or gender, so such traits may not be relied upon as clues.

The following is a story from my own past life memories. I was curious about a past life relationship with a male colleague that I knew in this lifetime. I wanted to know why we hit it off so well as friends while really having no romantic interest in each other, and so I decided to investigate a past life connection.

I discovered that I had once lived as a man during the Gold Rush. I recalled taking a journey from the Midwest, over the Rocky Mountains to California. I did not have great luck striking gold in California and began to head back east. Crossing the Colorado mountains, I came down into Central City where I met a fellow miner. He offered me shelter in his small cabin, and we became good friends. We were both solitary people leading a simple life, holding similar goals of striking it rich, so he asked me to stay. I lived there for the rest of my days.

Reviewing that lifetime helped me to see that this man and I had a history of friendship that was comfortable and trusting but not romantic in nature.

While observing past lives, it is common to recognize people who are also now present in your life. The subconscious mind can be programmed to guide your client to a time when he has shared a life with a specific person. In doing so, he may be able to discover a variety of relationships with one person over several lifetimes.

To direct a client to return to a lifetime where he may witness a relationship with a particular person, make suggestions to the subconscious mind during the induction and visualization, as demonstrated in the following example.

A client explained that her marriage had gone flat and that she was attracted to a man she knew at work. She wanted to experience a past life that would lend clarity to her relationship dilemma. Because two men were involved, I decided to address this issue by going to lifetimes that involved her husband, and then to other lifetimes that involved the second man.

In order to direct her mind toward a specific goal, I began by saying, "Ask the subconscious to take you to a lifetime that will help you understand your relationship with your husband. Where do you find yourself?"

My client answered, "I am in a tent; it is an Egyptian setting. I'm in the desert in what I believe is Saudi Arabia, Egypt, or India. We are at war. I am there with another man—he is my husband in this life. We are good friends and brothers, comrades engaged in a battle. We are scared but we're encouraging each other, trying to be brave. My friend went out from where we were sheltered and he was shot. I crawled out and pulled him back. He died in my arms. Now I see a cloud of dust going over us. Some of us are waking up. We're in a tent, and it's quiet. The battle is over. I am tired, and it's time to go back home. Everyone in our group is either dead or wounded. I'm wounded, too. I die much later, of cancer, at the age of 67."

I asked my client to go to a second lifetime involving her husband.

"I'm outside this time. It is green and beautiful. There is a hillside with an ocean in the distance. I see green, flowing grass. I have walked out of the house, which is built into the hillside. It's made of sod; it's dark and dank. I'm an old grandma and I have a large family; we all live together in this awful place. There is a wooden table with a bench. Everything is rustic. My grandson is there: he is my husband in this lifetime. He is so cute, so full of life, smiling and laughing. He's always in a good mood. Since his mother died I have cared for him like a son. He is the joy of my life. The two of us have a similar disposition, a positive attitude and a joy in life."

Now I ask the subconscious mind to take her to yet another lifetime, this time with the man she knows from work.

"I'm on a beach. It's sandy and the ocean crashes against the sand. I'm Polynesian, with long black hair. Maybe I'm Hawaiian or Indonesian. I have dark skin. I am laughing and I'm young. There is a get-together. There is a pig roasting. I see my friend. He's handsome, with a sparkle in his eye. We are drawn to each other; we flirt and fall in love. There is a ceremony. Now I see myself crying. I'm scared…scared of dying. There is a fire, I can smell it. The wind is blowing. There is a volcano erupting nearby and we couldn't get to the boat. We couldn't get away. Now the village is destroyed. It's terrible. We were incinerated alive. In that lifetime, I died clinging to my lover."

I ask my client how she would advise her past life counterpart. She tells her to let go of him.

"She lets go and there is a peace after that. It's just that I sense the heat and the screaming. It's terrible. She's so scared of it. Now she lets go and she's peaceful. It's better now. She's sad, but there is no pain."

We moved then to another lifetime with her friend from work.

"It's an igloo! How funny to be so cold after being burned! We are Eskimos. We have great dogs; maybe we are scientists, it seems we are conducting experiments. We are going somewhere to get supplies. It's so cold. I'm female and my friend is male. It's funny. We are kind of nerdy, brainy types. We love what we do and it's exciting. We are lovers. We weren't married in that life, but it felt to me as though we were committed to each other. Later we return home, and I discover that he has been cheating on me. He leaves me and my heart is broken. I had lived my life like a Pollyanna and this is a blow to my reality. I learn that things don't always work out as planned. I am so embarrassed. We have a mutual clique of friends, and it's awkward. The 'other woman' is blonde, funny, and gregarious. I was nerdy and plainer. I didn't want to be a part of that group of friends anymore. I'm embarrassed, hurt, and angry with him."

When asked what she learned from viewing that past life, my client exclaimed, "How you handle disappointment makes you what you are! Challenges are what make you stronger. When one door closes, another opens. The tragedies and disappointments in life build character. I may have enjoyed those lifetimes that came with a golden spoon, but they are not as enriching as those that require you to crawl through the foxholes."

My client received information in these regression sessions that empowered her to make clearer, more educated decisions concerning her marriage and friendships. She is now able to see the deeper facets of her relationships with each of the two men in question.

A person's choice of a mate and her ways of dealing with relationship issues can become clearer after visiting other lives. Your client may learn that the person she felt such a strong energy from and later married in this lifetime was a "villain" toward her in a previous lifetime. Perhaps she interpreted that intense energy as a sign of their deep connection and, in the period of infatuation, overlooked the fact that the energy's origin was a negative event. Similarly, the reason why someone else consistently triggers a volatile reaction in the client may become apparent when she observes her role with that person in previous lives.

Upon experiencing past life relationships with present life people, my clients often notice changes in the way they think and feel about the people around them. Once your clients have discovered other lifetimes that they shared with parents, siblings, friends, mates, or children, their understanding of the dynamics of these relationships becomes deeper and fuller. Regressions create a more holistic sense of our interpersonal relationships, and of the lessons that arise within those relationships. We find out ways in which we agreed before birth to assist each other in our life paths. With the understanding that each person we encounter may have been our parents, siblings, or spouses in other lifetimes, we come to recognize the precious nature of every human soul. Each one carries the potential of having served some important role in one or more of our own lifetimes. In this sense, we are all family.

Even encounters with strangers can take on a new dimension. Who knows whether they played a significant role in one of our past lives? The postman, grocery clerk, or doctor may have been your mother, your best friend, or the cause of your demise in another time and place. That person cutting you off in traffic may have been your endearing but rowdy best friend in a former incarnation, who is simply trying to get your attention again.

One of my clients wanted to have a deeper understanding about her relationships with her daughter and her dear friend. I asked her to close her eyes, breathe, and imagine a hallway. As she did so, she came to a rustic log door with a handle made of rope.

C: It's dark and I'm comfortable. I am in a crib that swings on a brass stand. If I move a little, I can make it rock. I am a female. I notice pink lace. I like the swing, maybe too much. I am happy. I like this space. I am not frightened. I have a nanny who wears a black uniform with crisp white things. Now I am on a rocking horse and I'm really going for it. I like the rocking motion. The nanny is my friend, maybe my teacher. I don't get to play with other children much. Maybe she is my governess. Now I am outside on a swing. I am going as high as I possibly can. She doesn't say I can't, but she makes sure that I don't get hurt. The swing hangs from a big tree. Sometimes I like to climb this tree.

ML: (continuing to ask questions to take her deeper into the experience) What is the next memorable event?

C: I am a teen now. I am being sent away to school, and I'm really sad. I don't want to be separated from my governess. I don't really know my parents. She is the one who has raised me and taught me everything that I know.

ML: Do you recognize her energy as similar to anyone you know in this lifetime?

C: She feels like my daughter in this life.

ML: What happens at school?

C: It is made of brick. It is cold and there are rules, bad teachers, and we sleep in a dorm. I have trouble socializing and conforming. I am unhappy, so I sneak away and take long walks. I sit by the river a lot; I write and sketch. Later when I am about 18 or 19 years old, I travel with my governess. We go to Greece to see the statues and buildings—all that we had looked at in books when I was growing up. She is still my best friend. We go to Rome. We giggle, laugh, and learn. I hate wearing the dresses; they are so hot.

ML: What is the year?

C: 1890.

ML: Where is home for you?

C: Edinburgh.

ML: Move ahead in time. What happens later in your life?

C: I have married and have two girls. The same governess lives with us, but she is too old to be their governess. She is more like a grandmother.

ML: What have you learned from viewing this past life?

C: Let your kids experience life and learn through those experiences. Learning is fun and it is a gift. Knowledge is power. I didn't want to be like my parents were in that lifetime. They had zero connection or affection for each other or for me.

ML: What was your governess' name?

C: Mary. She gave me the affection and connection that I needed.

ML: How will your knowledge of that life affect the one you're living now?

C: It shows me a deeper relationship with my daughter; it explains why we are so close now. She is so vibrant and eager to learn. Already, at six years old, she is her own person. I need to give her plenty of space and love. She will always have a solid personal boundary. Just because she runs off in one direction doesn't mean that she won't come back. There is always a place where she feels loved and accepted.

Whenever you meet someone with whom you will be closely involved—a potential mate, boss, child, in-law—it is wise and often extremely helpful to take the time to follow the memory of that energy back through the veils of time and discover the depth and true nature of the energy between you and this new person.

After experiencing a number of past life regressions, it is possible for your client to move closer to a sincere recognition that all the people who make up the humanity of this world are connected in some significant way. We have interacted with others in many forms, taking on various roles with each other throughout history. Our paths intersect again and again; we change roles as in a game of musical chairs.

One of my clients re-experienced a lifetime in which she was a little girl and her grandmother was dying. It was very upsetting to the little girl because she loved her grandmother so deeply. When I asked whether she recognized her grandmother as anyone she knew in this present life, my client said, "The energy feels like my son's."

In the same way that your clients may recognize various relationship roles they have played over time, when they regress to a variety of past lives, they have the opportunity to learn that they have been both males and females. Our spirits can choose which gender they will experience in a given lifetime. Some souls seem to prefer one or the other, and they therefore experience most lifetimes as one particular gender. When a spirit resonates with a specific sexual orientation, that trait may underlie his personality even during a lifetime in which he has come into a body of the opposite sex.

This may offer a possible explanation for homosexuality, for men who are effeminate or women who are masculine. Gender may be chosen to facilitate the fulfillment of a specific purpose, to make one sexually available or unavailable to a specific mate, or to provide an experience out of the norm for that soul. Gender may also be chosen purely for physical, genetic reasons, or for reasons of timing.

One of my clients was a young man, 19 years of age, whose mother had given him a gift certificate for a past life regression. She was present in the room during his experience.

As the young man went into trance and began the regression, his first words were that he was in excruciating abdominal pain. As the scene opened and he became aware of his surroundings, he exclaimed that he was a Native American female, squatting in her tepee, giving birth to her child. He went on to experience the childbirth and then returned to a state of calm comfort.

At the end of the session, we discussed how grateful his future wife would be because he now can be truly sympathetic while she is going through pregnancy and childbirth. Few men can relate to the childbirth experience as personally as this young man now can!

We have all experienced lives as people of different races, cultures, and religions, and as such, we have spoken a variety of languages. It is difficult to be prejudiced when you have experienced personal recall of a lifestyle or persecution very similar to another ethnic group. In this way, experiencing past life regressions encourages you to honor the divine that is common to every soul.

Occasionally, I have had clients of one race who, in the midst of a regression, suddenly exclaim that they are of a different race. They may be enchanted, looking at their skin or hair color. Some of my clients have experienced past lives in which their religious beliefs contrasted sharply with their current spiritual practice. Again, this gives them the opportunity to broaden their perceptions and experiences.

Marriage and Divorce

Past life regression often helps to explain challenges that cycle through a marriage and can bring clarity to certain aspects of a partner's character.

A woman came in for a regression in the midst of a divorce from her husband who had been unfaithful to her. (We will call him Tom.). Before moving on, she wanted to gain a deeper understanding of their relationship.

As she enters her memory of the past life, she discovers that she is the hired servant for a wealthy couple. She has lived with them since her birth. Her present husband, Tom, is her boss in that lifetime, and he is married. As the scene unfolds, he is teaching her to read by studying the Bible. This provides private time for the two, and she begins to fall in love with him. He takes advantage of her feelings and initiates an intimate, sexual relationship with her.

She says, "My heart races when I think about that original home. There is fear, adrenaline. I am so afraid of getting caught. I remember him pushing himself on me. I was scared...and not. The first time we had sex, it was in the bedroom. I was a virgin. I was 17 and scared. I liked it, too. But I don't like the fact that I like it. The whole idea makes me feel disgusted with myself, and guilty."

Wanting to help my client clear those feelings, I proceed with Object Imagery, asking her where she feels those emotions and sensations and asking her to describe them.

"It's in my chest," she says. "It is heavy. There is a hole being burned into my chest (Interestingly, this client had a mastectomy due to cancer.) It's a big black hole. It protects me from other people's opinions and from harm. It's uncomfortable. It doesn't work, but it is a part of me now. If it were gone, I would be lighter, freer, unburdened, unchained."

She says that her lesson from that life was: "Stand up for yourself. Take control of yourself. Be proud. Stand and be firm. Believe in yourself. Don't be afraid of rejection. It doesn't matter." Through visualization, my client imagines filling the hole in her chest with self-love.

Later in her former lifetime, she had moved on and done well for herself. She was operating her own drinking establishment and was enjoying life surrounded by friends. She was proud of her accomplishments.

It is interesting to note that, in the life this woman remembered, she had been the man's mistress. This time she was the wife, and the man still had a mistress. The roles had changed a bit, but the man's character had remained the same.

Childhood Abuse

I am frequently asked why a person chooses to come into a lifetime that results in childhood abuse. Later in the book we will look at this issue more closely. For now, read this fascinating narration by a client who remembered her experience beginning *between lifetimes* and on into her present incarnation. The segment vividly demonstrates the metaphorical nature of perception.

"The scene opens into deep, dark space. There is no landing. No stars. It's two-thirds open now. I'm not sure of going out there. It is a soft nothingness that would feel good on my skin. I wouldn't have to do anything, it's the ultimate hibernation.

"I want to let go. I let go. There is nothing, but I'm caught by an invisible puffiness. I'm not falling into oblivion. I wonder, did my subconscious set up the support? I'm passed from one place to another, bouncing gently. I lie down.

"A being comes, as though through cellophane. His face and hands come out through this membrane. Now I feel like I am being held in the branches of a tree. It's a solid tree, with firm branches, but I'm afraid they will break. It appears that a stork comes. There is a rattle shaped like a plastic safety pin. The stork is wearing a captain's hat. Am I a baby now?

"I am feeling a tugging at my pelvis. I'm being rocked by my limbs, in preparation to be born. It seems someone is saying that I've rested enough: 'It's time for her to get ready.' Huh? I feel like I'm coming out of a sleep. I start to sit up. I say, 'Where do you want me to go?' I resist what they are telling me. It's not easy. They are being soft with me.

"I start to panic and get rigid. I now seem to look like myself as an adult, with this body and face.

"There is a pulse of light and energy through the tree. It's getting me going. I'm being nudged away. It's hard; I'm really resistant. They want me to go away. They tell me, 'Sorry, it's time.' I'm baffled. What? Why?

"I notice a long tunnel. I'm being shown where I will be going. Oh, no, this does not bode well. I notice a striping, then stars. There is a light at the end. I notice fuzzy white or gray. I'm resisting so much; my body doesn't want this to be happening. There is a fuzzy light, and it comes toward me. Now I am sitting in a cloud. I'm still attached to the previous place. Someone reaches out from the clouds. They give me something to come into. I don't know what this is. Anyway, I let go of the tunnel. It's dark now. I'm in the clouds floating, in an angel outfit. "Someone points at the tunnel, reminding me I can't go back home. This is not good news for this body.

"I hear a message: 'You are going to go through a lot of paralyzing, overriding emotions. You'll forget who you are many times over. There will be glimmers that will seem like a speck. You will feel separate, abandoned, and lost. You will go in through your mother and not remember.'

"I'm thinking, 'My father is crazy.' My mother is reaching out to me. I can't believe I am being born to these extremely toxic people.

"I want my own voice. I shake my head silently. I resist. Now I'm here in this body. In that moment of transition, I forget. I'm sunshiny. I take on a vehicle of sunshine. I keep myself from crossing over into their world. Instead, it made them want me more. I do that so they think I am incredible and will want me. I want it on my terms.

"I am given over to my father by my mother. She knows we're connected. Energetically it feels bad and she's terrified, but she does it. My father takes me on as if I'm his trophy. He's waiting for me. I'm full of light. He wants me sexually. There is no time to grow up. No time. I'm given to him, like in other cultures. I'm two years old or less. There is no chance to get my bearings. I see my grandfather in the perimeter."

I ask my client to go back to before she connected with this body, before this started, and tell me what she noticed then.

She says, "Again, I'm in that tree. That being has facial features that are distinct and beautiful. It's attempting to help me. It's time for me to rest. I'm being jostled around. I'm flipped like a pancake. Why is that being so angry? It hurts to be prepared. It makes me wake up and get ready. My body is not happy. It's like being tortured, in a way, but I go along. I don't put up a fight.

"He is like my grandfather, but in that place he is so evil, so disgusting. I also notice another being in spirit form. He says, 'Look at this one. We got her. I told you we could do it. I wouldn't have believed it.'

"They were tracking me down. They are negotiating with each other for me. Who gave me up? I thought there was more to me. I let them pull me in. I thought I was tricking them. It seemed like a good deal. I thought I could do God's work, in disguise. I thought

I would let them think they got me. It was cruel for me to do that to myself. It was unfair. I set myself up to come into danger. That wasn't nice. What happened? Who lead me to this?

"I'm floating in space. The evil faces are uncloaked. They are watching, grinning. Who did this? It is not okay. Then the process begins. It's as though they are licking their chops. I see the tree there. It is a respite to me for strength and rest.

"They picked my mother. She wouldn't stop it. They were thinking, 'But you'll be of our lineage.' To me it is like being bacteria on a sponge. Someone was masquerading as God. Who sent me? Was it a false god?

"Now I'm experiencing happiness. I'm out of my body, but connected to a human form. It feels like maybe this took place in Atlantis. I'm drawn into a powerful vortex. I seem to come too close and then I am pulled in. I can't get out, I spin out of control. There is confusion. It's a whirlwind, down, down...I see my grandfather and then the tree. I'm dizzy...totally off center.

"I'm not supposed to be here, this is not good. I shouldn't have had to come through like this. I want out of this mess. I'm like Dorothy, with the evil witch. There are so many illusions and she tries so hard. Still she's taken from her home. I'll never be the same. My innocence was trashed, I'm trashed. Now a force wants to pull me off my path. This is not good.

"Through this I have learned that I can see well. Not a lot gets past me. I don't always choose to go with my intuition, but I generally know things. I carry my religion in my heart. I understand it somehow. I didn't die, and I won't die. And now I see why I have always felt I had to fight for my life. I understand an enormous amount about human motivation, greed, fear, and avarice. I see why certain things happen on this planet. A big piece was missing from my understanding, but now I understand. I am a spiritual being with compassion and depth. I can look at the dark beings. Sometimes there are evil beings and I can take a stance.

"I need to take my soul and hold it. I need to just hold it. I can feel the direct connection to God. It is never-ending. I need to be strong and energetic. I need a cellular healing so that I never fall prey to that energy. That was my weakness.

"It was not enough to know that I'm a high energy being. I need to surround myself with people who see me and adore me. I can grow, like a skyscraper. I need tenderness, nurturing. I need to be held. There is an exchange: the old for the new. I am giving up my entire way of looking at myself. People are lured to die before their time because of this force.

"The highlight of what I do is when I see people come alive by something I've done; I enjoy being able to see a shift in them. It gives them hope, a jump start, and motivation. Then they can go out and be, and do what they are to do. I'm a purpose activator: I wake people up when they are ready. My purpose is to populate the planet and help in the balance between those that are asleep and those that are awake. The world naturally heals without chaos."

This was an extraordinary case, not typical of the experiences my clients report when they remember being between lives. It is appropriate to be aware that all is not lightness and comfort in past life regressions.

Parenting and Adoption

The challenges of parenting can sometimes be resolved when parents witness past life relationships among family members. In the following case, there were extraordinary circumstances in the present life that set the scene for going back into the time between lives.

My client, a female in her teens, came for a session at her mother's request. The mother had adopted her at 18 months, and the teen was experiencing numerous behavioral problems. Both mother and daughter wanted to understand the root cause of their difficulties, and perhaps discover how to resolve them. We began the session by regressing back through the daughter's present life memories. Starting with deep relaxation techniques, I asked her to go back to her earliest memories.

She began by recanting memories about arguments witnessed between her birth mother and her grandmother. The relationship between her biological mother and father vacillated between the congenial and the volatile. She recalled being left in a closet as an infant while her mother left the house from when it was sunny until after dark.

She also remembered an incident when her birth father came home with a gun. The conversation led her to believe that he tried to kill someone. Eventually he was arrested. She also had memories of drugs, and of her mother dressing up at night when her father told her to go to work.

The daughter reported some happy memories as well, of her father smiling and telling her that everything would be all right. She was adopted after her birth parents were incarcerated.

Then I asked her to go back further, to the time before she was born, to discover what she might know about that time. Here is what she reported: "Someone has a hand on my back and he is pointing to two people. He says, 'If you go down there, you can help them.' They have tried before and couldn't conceive. They don't want to adopt. Having me as their baby would be good for them and for me. It would be good for me because there is someone waiting for me. It isn't them, but someone else. He says, 'These people are to have you.' There is some difficulty in life that I needed to fix for them. He tells me, 'Don't be scared, whatever happens. Always be happy. They may not be perfect, but they need someone in their lives.'

"I regretted it at first; I didn't want to leave where I was. But he told me that I had to go. He said they would bring me something that I needed. I had to be with them. There was a plan for me, something waiting for me. When I asked him about that, he said that there had been a mistake and it needed to be fixed. When I asked what that had to do with me, he told me they are a part of me. They tell me that it will help me in my life. It will help me to be someone very different. He said they would help me through it. They know what's going on and what would happen. They say there is a dark force trying to hurt me. They never told me what it was. If I don't do this, I will be here forever. He wanted to help these other people, so I said I would do it."

This young lady had a rough start in her present incarnation. With this deeper understanding about her pre-birth decisions and of her early childhood experiences, she was given the opportunity to strengthen herself and to stay focused on the bigger picture.

Soul Groups

During a two-year period, together with a group of several dozen peers, I engaged in a research project involving past life regression. We paired up on a regular basis to facilitate regressions for each other, targeting specific periods in time. We would change partners and collect information on several lifetimes in many situations.

We discovered that we had frequently incarnated together. Apparently we are all members of two soul groups who continually help each other through our various incarnations. During the regressions, we consistently recognized each other in those former lifetimes: as brother, sister, mother, or boss. With no prior knowledge of these findings, another person in a separate, private session would recognize the same relationship as well. Through these independently performed regressions, we were able to corroborate the memories of several different people concerning events, relationships, conditions, scenery, customs, clothing, and more.

Frequently, being with your soul group is a major consideration when choosing a body in which to incarnate. Because you are connected energetically to your soul mate and to those in your soul group, whatever effects them energetically will affect you as well.

If members of your soul group are slowing down their progress, perhaps beginning to slide toward oblivion or extinction, that backward movement will exert an energetic pull on you, creating a drag on your spiritual growth. If you notice that members of your soul group are experiencing difficulties or are, alternatively, engaged in a quest that interests you, you may feel compelled to be born into a body that will place you close by. Sometimes your attachment to someone is so great that you will overcome any obstacle so that you may experience, once again, the physical sensations and pleasures you have shared with this person in previous lives.

The case studies presented above provide a general look at the broad variety of benefits available to your client through past life regression. If you provide a sense of openness and curiosity, your client's subconscious will provide answers, giving him access to parts of himself and his experience that otherwise might have taken many years of present-time soul searching. Past life regression and between-life memories places one's life experience in the larger context of a universal quest for spiritual evolution.

Experiencing past lives and life between lives shows you that you are not just a personality at the mercy of a random fate. Rather, you are a soul who seeks out specific experiences for the purpose of expanding your spiritual understanding.

CHAPTER TWO
Why We Forget

Clients frequently ask, "If past life memories are supposed to be available to us, then why do we forget them?" Some who pose this question have come to feel that past life exploration is taboo. Nevertheless, getting the full picture of your soul's journey is not only your innate right, it is also vital to your self-awareness and growth. You have experienced every moment of your journey. It is a record of your own life; it cannot be taken away from you. So why do we choose to forget?

There are three main causes of amnesia concerning past lives.

Life's Distractions

Children may remember a great deal of past life information when they are very young. Yet imagine for a moment what their experiences are.

While in the womb a soul may be fully conscious of his past lives, his soul's essential purpose, and his reasons for coming into a given life. The moment of birth, however, is tremendously stressful, sometimes even life-threatening for both mother and child. On emerging from the womb, the baby enters a period of adjustment to the physical body: bright lights, chilly air, learning to drink mother's milk, and having people handle him.

Later the child may encounter the uncomfortable surprise of jealous siblings and the kindness of doting grandparents, as well as the difficulty of communicating desires and needs in a world where most of the inhabitants are not telepathic!

Fast forward ahead a couple of years, through learning to operate the physical body, grabbing, sitting, standing, walking, and finally forming the first words that are coherent to his caretakers. By the time the child is able to communicate verbally, much of his pre-birth knowledge is already locked in hidden chambers of the subconscious mind.

Societal Norms

Around the age of four, the child may begin to communicate the remnants of his memories of an entirely different lifetime or lifetimes. These communications may be ignored, or the child may be patronized. "A nice story," he is told. "Now run along and play."

Without encouragement or support, past life memories recede into the shadows of the subconscious, like shameful acts. Years later, those who are curious may end up investing considerable time and money just to recover the memories that are their birthright.

Although most spiritual belief systems include some version of an afterlife, in some cultures past life memories are denounced as unreal or evil. Thus many people are discouraged from learning, during this lifetime, about the past experiences that have contributed to their present selves.

Avoidance

Sometimes people forget experiences of other lifetimes to escape negative memories. Reactions of shame, horror, regret, remorse, fear, boredom, or grief can all bring about such forgetfulness. Have you ever met someone who believed that death would bring an end to all her troubles? She says things like: "It will all be over when I'm dead," or "We're born with a clean slate."

Everyone has painful memories. Haven't you had your heart broken, lost a loved one, suffered a painful physical injury, or said or did something you deeply regret? These trying experiences are part of the human condition. Not only are they natural to your journey, but they also measure your character by presenting tests and lessons that allow you to mature as a soul. In the midst of a crisis, you tend to examine your choices and behaviors more closely, seek more creative solutions, and strengthen your character in ways that do not occur when things are easy.

All too frequently many of us take the attitude that it is best to leave the past behind: it is more comfortable to bury memories than draw them out. When we allow our memories to go underground, however, we miss the valuable lessons they have to offer.

I frequently see clients who cling fervently to memories of their most difficult experiences, using those experiences to define themselves and their outlook on life. There is an analogy I often use when encountering this mindset.

Consider a bodybuilder who works out diligently, undergoing periods of stress and strain on a regular basis in order to mold his physique in very specific ways. Yet when his exercise session is over, the body builder puts the weights down and simply enjoys the results. If you exercise our character through the weight of experience, you, too, can use your heavy times to build a firm foundation of wisdom. Unfortunately, you may forget to put down the weights, and instead you continue to drag stress and trauma into the future, unable to enjoy the results of all your hard work.

Through past life regression you can become fully aware of old burdens that you may still be carrying. If you continue to lug these with you from lifetime to lifetime, they result in stress, pain, blockage, phobias, and dysfunction at every level. Conversely, when you heal the residue of these past life episodes, you leave them in their rightful places, and you bring along only the wisdom and growth accumulated by having lived and learned through those events.

When you seek to heal issues that persist from other incarnations, it becomes easier to do the same with the episodes and experiences of your present lifetime. As new traumas and stresses occur, your goal is to have at your disposal the wisdom and the tools to release them, so that you do not carry dead weight into the future.

≈

I have worked with people who resisted going into a past life out of fear that they might discover they had committed some atrocity. They dreaded finding out that they had murdered or raped someone, or that they had cheated or lied. Just as their unethical behavior caused problems in a past life, their great efforts to hide it may continue to cause problems for them now.

When people die, they do not automatically transform from a negative orientation to a positive one. Their character remains intact. Thus if a client is avoiding something in the reality of her character, trying to hide from the error of her ways, she may not be able to face these truths even from the vantage point of a new body and lifetime. To see yourself fully, or not to see yourself fully: the choice is yours.

Every day the newspapers are filled with stories of people who do all manner of harm to one another. After death, those who have made poor choices find themselves between lifetimes, presented with yet another opportunity to reincarnate.

Over time, and through a variety of experiences, a soul learns the lessons necessary to change negative character traits. Many of us, on venturing back into our other lifetimes, remember committing acts about which we now feel ashamed. The fact that we now regret those behaviors indicates that growth has been accomplished in the interim.

In a profound series of past life memories, one of my clients was able to reveal the source of her present-life issues, which included multiple physical ailments as well as negative emotions and troublesome dreams. She had been prescribed medication for anxiety, and was referred to my office by a medical doctor who understood that she needed something beyond what he was offering her.

This woman had been brought up with a strong fundamentalist Christian background and was not at all confident that she had experienced past lives. She also suspected that undergoing hypnosis and attempting to visit her past lives might be a sin.

Although she was somewhat apprehensive, she also felt compelled to get to the root of her various disorders, visions, and negative emotions.

The regression that follows contains material that may be offensive to some. I have included portions of it here to show the profound understanding and healing that can emerge from working with past lives. During the session, I directed my client to ask for assistance from any spirit guides who might be present, and at a certain point she makes mention of a guide advising her as she reconsiders the past lifetime.

As we begin the regression, my client describes being on her deathbed in a previous life. As we examine her memories of the events leading up to this moment, she begins to recall. "I was an unconventional man, about 37 years old. I think I was German, and I performed experimental, hideous medical procedures for the Nazis. I was very brave, a doctor. I would stand up against them. The nurse tells me, 'You thought that you were the reincarnation of something evil, not just brave. But you kept us alive. You saved lives. You were brave. I want to help you through all your lifetimes. To help you with the things that you are required to do. You prayed for them before they died. You would cover them.'"

As my client continued to recall her lifetime as a Nazi doctor, she observed that her past life counterpart would medicate his nurse so that she could tolerate the atrocities that she, too, was facing. The nurse herself was subjugated to a variety of abuses at the hands of a German officer.

Commenting on that lifetime, my client continued: "I could have left, but I wouldn't have known the exhilaration of scientific discovery that would help the world in many ways. I wasn't evil, but I was there. I could be guilty. She (the nurse) tells me I shouldn't hold it so deeply. My health problems in this life are from that time. There is no need for the anxiety and fear. She said I was brave. I have such a depression. It is like a vice squeezing my chest and head. It comes from the memories. These symptoms are present because I have to remember, and I have to repent. I remember the blood. I see myself operating on a man in third level starvation. He had scurvy and rickets. I operated on his brain with no anesthesia. His eyes watched me as I removed part of his brain. I was possessed with the quest for knowledge. People were expendable. They look like sheep to me. I hate myself. I thought I was one of God's chosen, and I did this. 'I will never die,' I thought, 'I will live forever.'

"We thought the Jews had a special cell within them, an entity that made them so strong. We never found it. We took living tissue, cells, and put them in other people and animals. We would do complete lobotomies to desensitize the pain. We only had primitive life sustaining systems and manual operations. We made some of the people keep others alive. When I see the stories now, I feel I was a monster. Some of the people that I worked with then, I know now. They are the same now. My spirit guide says that I have to part with them. I never had any friends in that life. I only had my work. I didn't want friends. I was obsessed. I remember laughing and having a drink one day, with blood under my fingernails. Sometimes I would see people and know what it would be like for them to die. I would look at people's hands to see if they had blood under their nails. I would chew my nails so there would be no blood. I could cut someone open and perform surgery if I had to, right now. Not to hurt them, but because I could. I can tell what's wrong with people now.

"I was a doctor before that, too. That was in the 1700s. In that life, I died on the battlefield of a gangrenous infection with a bullet in my shoulder. It was hot the day I died. I hated the heat. I saw the bloody mess that I left behind. There had been a skirmish on the border between Germany and Austria. I was English. I heard about it and I went to help. My wife begged me not to go, but I left her and my two children at home. In this life, I have a husband like that, who goes his own way. I hate him for that. Now I know how she feels.

"I just want God to know that I am sorry for all the despicable acts that I was involved in. I had no conscience. I was so enthusiastic about science. I have been punished this lifetime. I feel more than I should now. It is atonement, and I'm sorry. Now I wouldn't take anyone's life, for any reason. Then (in the Nazi lifetime) I had some fear, but I was brave and outspoken. People were afraid of me, and they are afraid even now. Those people I performed experiments on would have been killed anyway. But that doesn't make it right. If God could only know . . . I wanted the scientific knowledge more than anything. I just couldn't wait for technology in order to learn it in a dignified manner."

***

Although we may not all have had such horrendous experiences in our past lives, chances are good that each of us has done something that has brought on a sense of shame or regret. Such feelings are counterproductive to the extent that they prevent growth. There are two ways to approach this dilemma.

If your client is afraid that a negative characteristic is going to surface during the past life regression, she may already be aware of a feature of her personality that needs to be examined and changed. On the other hand, some clients fear a negative trait will be revealed in the regression even when they know that they would not be capable of such behavior now. In this case, the client may be intuiting a past negative behavior that his soul has outgrown.

If you sense that your client is blocking or denying a negative emotion or that behavior is being blocked or denied, it will be important to help him face the character flaw and correct it as soon as possible. Blocking painful or frightening memories requires a tremendous amount of energy. This in turn creates stress, which may lead to premature aging and disease. Furthermore, until the root cause has been resolved, there remains a risk that the client will act on his blocked negative behaviors and emotions, creating another round of suffering for himself and others.

In my early years facilitating past life memories, a lovely, spiritually oriented woman came to my office for a regression. As she went into trance, she became very curious about her experience. She described sneaking down an alley. Gradually she realized that she was actually stalking someone. She then perceived, to her horror, that she had been a serial killer, much like Jack the Ripper. My client was obviously astonished at her memories as they unfolded more clearly in her mind.

After this regression, our discussion centered on the fact that she abhorred the memory. Since my client would never have considered such behavior in her present life, it was important to encourage her to observe the lessons of that experience and to appreciate the growth she had accomplished since that life.

Without knowing the background of a criminal character, we cannot understand how his mindset developed. Was he tortured as a child? Was he possessed by a demonic spirit? Did he have a chemical imbalance that caused his aberrant behaviors? The holistic counselor must gather a host of information to back up her assessment of people and their behaviors—and also her own!

Reframing: Opening the Door to Self-Acceptance

Duke Ellington said it best: "I merely took the energy it takes to pout and wrote some blues."

Reframing alarming memories can help your client appreciate her soul's evolvement. A wise counselor will encourage a client to measure the distance she has come in the course of her life experiences since performing the regrettable action. Reframing also involves extracting the learning, wisdom, and other benefits she may have derived from past life experience, thereby placing those memories in a more constructive light. It may not change the client's memories, but reframing helps her to view her actions from the larger perspective of the learning that takes place over the course of numerous incarnations.

A quick technique to introduce reframing into the session is to ask your client in what way did the experience benefit him with wisdom, skills, knowledge, or strengthened character traits.

Techniques for Reframing are covered more fully in *Hypnotherapy: A Client Centered Approach*.

CHAPTER THREE

How We Remember

Techniques for Past Life Regression

Past life recall may be achieved in several ways. Some people are able to revive memories of other lifetimes spontaneously, by watching a movie, reading a book, viewing a painting, visiting a location, or having a dream. Some are able to regress themselves during meditation or while writing in a journal. The trained regression therapist will also have a number of methods for facilitating past life regression for clients.

There are times when a client enters a past life spontaneously during a hypnosis session. If her belief system does not include the concept of reincarnation, she may interpret her visions as a metaphor or simply a figment of her fertile imagination. Either interpretation can be useful. A fundamental purpose in discovering past lives is to determine how the information gleaned can improve the client's well being during the course of the present life. A metaphor derived from the experience can give the person ample useful information. The lessons that are presented in the metaphor can be applied to the present life, providing valuable wisdom for the client.

While there are many ways to uncover past life memories, formal hypnosis will prove to be one of the most reliable. Having a qualified hypnotherapist as a guide, the client will enter a medium to deep trance and explore memories in a safe, supportive environment.

If difficult memories or patterns of dysfunctional behavior come to the surface while discovering past life information, you as facilitator should be equipped with techniques to rapidly resolve and heal them.

Although I will list formal steps in past life regression, most sessions are tailored to the circumstances and the client. Therefore, use these suggestions as a guideline.

Build rapport with the client

It is important that you and your client have a relaxed, trusting relationship. Rapport may be enhanced by energy, environment, language, eye contact, body language, and so forth. Where the client does not feel comfortable with the facilitator, the session is likely to be inhibited.

Use soft, flowing, neutral music

Avoid using music that is from a specific era or culture. A wide range of new age music is available that is very conducive to a session. Some of this music includes rhythmic tones that enhance trance states. The music should be slow and relaxing rather than lively or intense. A session can be quite successful even without music.

Discuss the client's goals for the session

Determine what it is that the client wants to achieve. This will help you determine how you will approach the language of the induction and the session.

Begin the induction and move into the regression

You may induce by progressive relaxation or any other method that helps the client achieve relaxation and focused attention. If the goal of the session is to discover the roots of a pain or emotion, you can easily achieve a past life regression using Object Imagery, as described in Chapter 8.

Before conducting past life regressions, it is recommended that a counselor have a thorough understanding of the techniques presented in *Hypnotherapy: A Client-Centered Approach*.

Create a safe space

It can be advantageous to guide a client to establish a safe space before proceeding into a past life. Creating a safe space can encourage a deeper state of relaxation and trust, as the client engages his imagination in an activity that has no right or wrong answers. The safe space also gives the client a haven to return to if the past life memories involve situations that are frightening or painful. Returning to the client's own safe space is also a gentle, comforting way to end a session.

Speak slowly

It is important to be very patient as you deliver the induction and while waiting for the client's response. Some clients take a long time to discover the answers to your questions, while others are able to respond quite quickly. Let the client set the pace. Remember that recovering a memory can feel like gradually picking up the torn remnants of a photograph, one by one, until the whole picture is seen. While you wait through long silences as the client gradually assimilates her experience, a minute may seem a lot longer to you than it does to her. An attitude of quiet, supportive patience on your part contributes greatly at such times.

Script for Past Life Regression

The following script can be used, or modified to suit the needs of your client.

Closing your eyes, take a deep breath. As you release your breath, release the tension in your muscles. With each breath in, draw in energy from the universal source. With each exhale, release tension and any concerns for the activities of the day. Turn your attention inward. Relaxing, deeper and deeper.

I wonder if you can imagine locating that still point within you, that place within you where you are at peace. Connecting fully with that still point within you, allow yourself to relax as deeply as you are comfortable doing, knowing only you can allow yourself to go deeper and deeper.

And now, I wonder if you can imagine your favorite safe space. It might be a place where you have been, where you felt at ease, or it might be a place you create in your imagination. And as you imagine this safe space, you begin to look around and explore your surroundings. What do you notice here at this time?

As you continue to explore your surroundings, you discover an especially nice spot where it would be so comfortable to sit down and relax. As you settle into this comfortable place, you realize that it has a special energy. In this place, you are connected to vast wisdom and knowledge. In this place, you are fully aware of how to go into the deepest trance state of meditation that you have ever experienced, knowing that only you can make that happen. Going there now, as I count from five to one. Five, going deeper and deeper. Four, feeling so good to relax and release. Three, feeling so relaxed, yet so curious. Two, going all the way down, now. One. That's right. Feeling so good.

As your body continues to relax and your mind goes even deeper, begin to envision a hallway stretching out before you. As you begin to move down along that hall, you notice the texture of the floor beneath your feet, and the color of the walls. There are doorways along this hall, each one leading to a past life experience that will be so helpful for you at this time. As I count from three to one, you will find yourself in front of one of these doors. Three, two, one. And how would you describe the door that you are standing in front of?

(Allow the client to describe the door. This gives permission to be creative and imaginative in a setting that has no right or wrong answers.)

When you are ready to step through that door, it opens and you move over the threshold. As you do so, do you find yourself indoors or outdoors? Describe the environment. As you explore this place, what else do you notice?

(Continue, slowly, with other questions that will assist your client in staying focused and moving through past life memories. You may ask questions about clothing, location, date, age, gender, activities, relationships, marriage, children, the age at death, and so forth.)

Throughout the regression session, encourage your client to be curious and inquisitive. Case studies included here can generate ideas about questions you may want to ask during a session to elicit additional details from your client's memory. Form your questions based closely on the information that the client offers; this will enhance your rapport and will allow the session to move smoothly, coherently, and intuitively.

For instance, you may respond to a client who comments, "All I see is darkness," in a number of related ways. "What qualities does that darkness have?" "What else do you notice about that darkness?" "How do you feel as you find yourself there?" "As you become accustomed to that darkness, what else do you begin to discern?" "Move ahead in time until something changes. What do you notice next?" and so on.

Other Factors in Past Life Regression

Metaphor

A metaphor is a symbolic image meant to correlate to, or substitute for, something else. Metaphor can be useful in helping a client understand or alleviate a pain or sensation (Object Imagery). When your client imagines herself in a particular place or time or wearing a particular costume, it can help create a safe distance from emotion-laden past (or present) life experiences, which might otherwise prevent her from accessing her memories. Metaphor, the process of comparing two dissimilar things so that they appear similar, can help your client gain valuable insights regarding specific people, places, talents, and experiences.

Associated and dissociated perspective

Clients may experience a past life from the perspective of being inside the body of the person they were in a previous lifetime (associated), or they may view the regression as though they are watching a film or remembering a dream (dissociated). It is not terribly important which perspective they choose.

Experiencing the past life regression from the associated perspective is most common, and the client is more connected to the memories, responses, emotions, and physical sensations elicited by those memories. Staying in the dissociated perspective during the regression, however, may be a way to gain a safe distance from the unpleasant emotions or events that a client is apprehensive about remembering from a first-person perspective. It is also possible that a client experienced a trauma during the past life that caused him to dissociate at the time, and so now he remembers it from a dissociated (out-of-body) perspective. When a client remains dissociated throughout a session, I usually ask him, out of curiosity, whether he also experiences his present life in this manner. An affirmative response may indicate the need for further counseling.

One of my clients was curious about her past lives and wanted to experience one of them. At the time she had no further agenda except to discover who she might have been in another lifetime. In the opening scene, she described a peaceful setting with grass, trees, and a pond of water behind her.

She continued, "In front of me is an older woman in a wheelchair. She is in her 80s or 90s. She is wearing black. She is being pushed by another female wearing burgundy-colored clothing. They are quiet. It has a proper feeling. The older woman wears glasses, and something with lace around her face. She is sweet, yet tired."

When asked what her relationship was to these women, my client responded that the older woman was her grandmother and that she herself was the other female, a little girl of seven years, pushing the wheelchair. She had begun the session by describing the scene from a peripheral (dissociated) viewpoint.

I asked her to associate with the body by saying, "Allow yourself to step into the body of the little girl so that you feel her body and are looking out of her eyes. What do you notice next?" From then on she remained associated with the body, experiencing the emotions, actions, and events from the perspective of the seven-year-old.

Anchoring

Anchoring can be used at the beginning of the session to instill confidence, courage, or creativity. Any resource that the client may need during the session can be planted at the beginning through the use of an anchor and returned to throughout the session. Further, if your client visits a past lifetime during which she had a resource or attribute that she would like to bring back with her into this lifetime, anchoring the desired state can powerfully accomplish that.

To anchor a positive state before the session begins, you may ask the client to return to a memory from this lifetime: a time when she experienced success, overcame a challenge, or had a breakthrough. As she recalls that event, have her consciously amplify the feelings elicited by the experience. In the midst of her vivid recollection, create an anchor by having her perform a physical motion, such as touching two fingers together, rubbing her hands together, or placing her hand over her heart.

Once you have asked the client to connect with the desired feelings by recalling a time when she vividly felt that way, you can also create an anchor by asking her subconscious mind to provide an imaginary symbol that represents the desired feeling. (In *Hypnotherapy: A Client-Centered Approach*, I refer to this as the Empowerment Symbol.)

At any time throughout the session, the client's anchor may be called upon to remind her of her courage, confidence, or other positive qualities.

Learning about the client

In addition to the messages that past life experiences reveal to our clients, the sessions also give us, as facilitators, valuable information about the clients themselves. How someone processes information during a session provides important clues about how we can best serve his needs therapeutically.

You may learn a great deal about your client's mental processes by observing his responses to the regression experience. You might look for the following:

- Does his mind race and fail to quiet down?
- Does he shy away from any painful situation?
- Does his mental screen go blank?
- Does he have difficulty making decisions?
- Does he notice and embellish minute details?
- Does he arrive at a certain point and get stuck?
- Does he view the process from a dissociated (third-person) perspective?
- Does he see the broad scope of the lifetime, but remain uninterested in the details?
- Does he try to control the session rather than allowing it to flow naturally?
- Does he analyze information even before his ideas have time to develop?
- Is he reluctant to believe any past life experience in which he appeared more powerful than his current image of himself?

How we ourselves go about our observations can be every bit as fascinating as our client's process of past life discovery. There are many ways to achieve a past life regression even when the mind is busy, the body will not relax, or an analytical part of the self will not yield. Rather than confronting these personality traits directly, you will learn how to solicit the client's assistance in overcoming these obstacles to retrieving past life memories.

The Scientific Method and Beyond

The scientific method of research and discovery is considered the best method available for discerning truth and reality. It works well for many types of objects and events. But the scientific method has its limitations. It can only measure and detect that which it is designed to measure and detect. Anything outside that scope will go unnoticed and unexamined. Too often, whatever falls beyond that scope is dismissed as unreal or irrational.

If we were to describe our world using only numbers, we would have to say that "independence" was not real. No numbers can describe or detect independence, therefore it cannot exist, right? Therein lies the problem. When we at last become able to develop methods of proof capable of measuring the mystical, then spiritual experiences will be deemed "real." Meanwhile, we must do the best we can to experience the extraordinary, make sense of the magical, and integrate the reality of possibility into our understanding.

To do so requires imagination and belief.

Imagination

My clients often say they don't have an imagination. It may be underdeveloped or stifled, but everyone has an imagination. Without it we would be unable to communicate. When your dining companion says, "Pass the ketchup," you reach out, grab the ketchup, and hand it to her. What, you may ask, has that got to do with imagination?

First, your mind perceived the request for ketchup, then it used your imagination and memory to draw a mental picture of something corresponding to the word *ketchup*. You looked around and found in your immediate vicinity an object that most closely matched the picture you had imagined. Perhaps it was sitting right in front of you on the table. At that point, your mind went on to imagine the act of grabbing the bottle and handing it over to your friend. Finally, your body executed the action. All of these steps, of course, are accomplished in a second or two, and there are many more steps that the brain instantaneously performs in order to complete this simple act, steps which are described in great detail in some of the hefty volumes found in medical libraries. The point is that we all use the imagination on a daily basis.

Here we are concerned with expanding the basic skill of imagining into something grander and more adventuresome: to encourage our clients' openness to their past life experiences and to fully claim their current life experiences.

Strategies to Expand and Exercise the Imagination

Practice creative visualization

You can have clients practice using their imagination by listening to guided visualization audiotapes and CDs. Encourage your client not to be passive in the process, but to really embellish the journey, adding details, emotions, curiosity, and surprises. Audio visualizations are widely available from your favorite book and music sources. Some libraries make such resources available at no charge. Audio CDs by this author are listed at the back of this book.

Read and make up stories

Reading science fiction stories requires a fertile imagination. This genre of tales involves characters, landscapes, vehicles, machinery, and adventures that have rarely if ever been seen or experienced in this world. Some people consider reading science fiction a waste of time, but it can be a valuable tool in expanding the imagination. Reading anything that takes us out of the bounds of the usual and into unexplored territory can help exercise our capacity to imagine.

You may have your clients practice writing fictional stories featuring outlandish characters in elaborate environments. Allow the story to stretch beyond all reasonable possibility: the wilder, the better. Encourage your clients to avoid limitations and judgments concerning style in this exercise.

Ask your clients to volunteer to tell stories to their children, their nieces and nephews, their grandchildren, or their friends' children. Telling imaginative stories can be great fun: your client may become the children's hero for delighting them with flights of fancy. Naturally, you will want to encourage your clients to make their stories age appropriate.

Belief

Belief is not the act of suspending our powers of reason, nor does it involve adhering to a philosophy or perspective at odds with all other accepted knowledge. Belief is a final leap of faith off the high mountain of reasoning, truth, facts, and substantiated evidence. When all the information you have collected about something points to the probability of a fact that cannot be proven by any other means, then belief is a reasonable next step. Belief is at the core of most scientific discovery and invention.

Belief is important to the experience of a past life because our belief systems act as filters of our experiences of reality. Expanding the familiar range of our beliefs can readjust the filters in helpful ways, so that we live more fully and express ourselves more expansively. Remember, there is always much more to the universe than has yet been discovered.

There was a time when the idea of the world being a round globe rather than a flat plane was beyond belief for the majority of people. Not so long ago, it was commonly believed that human beings would never be able to fly, and certainly they would never reach the moon. Yet space vehicles carrying teams of people now travel far beyond the moon. Once it was believed that the atom was the smallest particle in the universe. We now possess instruments that penetrate many steps beyond that, deep into the world of the microcosm. All of these inventions and advancements came about due to someone's curiosity, imagination, and belief, all coalescing around a particular subject.

I do not mean to suggest that we should believe in anything and everything, for that would make us gullible and foolish. Rather, I suggest remaining open to possibilities that lie outside the realm of ordinary experience, especially when such exploration is reasonable and harmless. Encourage your clients to study materials that help them stretch beyond accustomed ways of thinking and to listen open-mindedly to the experiences of others. Remaining open to undiscovered possibilities increases our odds of attaining personal proof in the realms of as yet uncharted experience.

When a person denies belief in something, she can still experience it, however, her perception of the experience may be altered. If a person doesn't believe in UFOs, for example, a certain flash of light and period of time missing from her memory may be interpreted as evidence of a stroke or, perhaps, food poisoning. Some out-of-the-ordinary experience has occurred, but its interpretation is determined by the personal beliefs, the filters, of the person having the experience.

Some people claim to have a broad belief system and an open mind; yet it is wise even for them to practice suspending disbelief in order to receive new information. Nature alone is radically amazing. In one evening of television viewing on a nature channel, it is possible to witness creatures and phenomena as strange as anything in science fiction. If such things can be captured on film, imagine what is yet to be discovered!

To practice suspending disbelief, have your client practice giving herself permission to experience whatever vision or thought comes her way, *without judgment or criticism*. She may receive useful information, or she may find herself dwelling in thoughts that seem to be pure nonsense. Until the client allows herself to observe the scope of mental data available, however, she is unlikely to uncover anything new, either within or without. Once your client gets better at witnessing the information she is taking in (without ruling it out due to judgment or internal criticism), she will be better able to examine the information she receives through past life regression. She will then be empowered to determine how much of that information is valuable to her.

CHAPTER FOUR
False Memory, Real Memory and Filters

A client experiencing regression for the first time may wonder whether the visions and sensations he had during the session were actual memories or merely stories conjured up by the imagination. It is easy to understand this reaction. In most cases, clients have little definitive proof of the validity of their past life memories, so they may find it a challenge to anchor them in reality with any certainty.

Doing repeated regressions to the same lifetime can help a client accept and integrate his past life experiences, and also provide more in-depth perspective on the information. In a series of such regressions, you may guide your client to discover details that might otherwise remain unknown: about customs, geography, or any data relevant to his current therapeutic issues. Later, your client may want to research the past life information at the library or online, thus providing proof that will help him make use of the remembered past life material.

Inauthentic memories do sometimes surface, however, often due to some unconsciously volunteered detail or leading question from the facilitator to which the client acquiesces out of an equally innocent desire to please the counselor. To avoid false memory recall, it is important that the facilitator use neutral language in the sessions. Open-ended questions such as those given below will elicit new information without leading the client's experience.

- What do you notice? What do you observe?
- What happens next? And then what?
- What do you know about that?
- Where are you? What is the date?
- Here are some leading questions to avoid.
- Is he your father?
- Is that celebration for your birthday?
- Are you angry about that?
- Do you think you were the President?

It is as important not to assume knowledge of another person's past life experience or emotions as it is not to assume we know what he feels or thinks at the present time. In the same vein, the client experiencing a regression must avoid drawing conclusions about his experience based on books, movies, or other materials. Encourage him to remain open to what it is, rather than adjust his memory to his expectations.

In the realm of memory, there is plenty of room for error. Take caution in accepting a client's memories of another lifetime at face value. Keep working over time to help him to fill out details, verify his past life role, and gain the full measure of wisdom available from his experience.

To demonstrate to your client the general unreliability of information gleaned from memory, you may want to ask him to describe—with complete accuracy—what he was doing two weeks ago last Thursday. Ask him for the exact time of day of this memory, and press for details about the people, places, conversations, and emotions. Unless some catastrophic event occurred at that time which caused your client to become hyper-alert, he will probably find himself struggling to recall details even of these recent events. Aside from deep trauma or the heights of ecstasy, most people recall only vague data, patterns, and general impressions, even of very special occasions in their lives.

Encourage your client to be patient with his memory. Remind him to relax and give himself some latitude in remembering events, occupations, and relationships that occurred 100, 500, or even 1,000 years ago, separated from today by many deaths and births.

Some people are blessed with remarkable powers of recall and can vividly remember minute details of their past lives. The majority, however, typically retrieve a general understanding of their past life occupations, marriages, and number of children, as well as the location and a sense of the era. Even these apparently vague details can be used to discover life lessons and correlations between the client's past incarnation and the present one.

So how can we determine that the client's memories are real? It is difficult ever to be completely certain. All of our memories are subjective. The mental data we think of as "memories" are mostly our perceptions of events, and are therefore colored by all of the experiences and beliefs that preceded them.

Most memory, therefore, can be considered "false memory"—even if we are recalling what happened last week. If you remember the strategies of a past life battle, do not jump to the conclusion that you were the general leading the charge. You may have been a right-hand man, closely identified with the general's personal ambitions and strategies. If you remember yourself as royalty, it may be true that you were the queen, but you may also have been the cousin who was invited to all the court activities or the sister who wished, and often fantasized, that she was queen.

Through past life recall, one woman remembered the Camelot years and, more precisely, life on the Isle of Avalon. She recalled the ceremonies, politics, and lifestyle. She also remembered being in love with Lancelot and practicing magical rites. She thus concluded that she had once lived as Morgan LeFey. It made sense, and she had bountiful informational details that seemed to support that claim. However, upon further regressions to that same lifetime, she discovered instead that she had been one of Morgan's several sisters.

Such mistaken identity is understandable. The two women shared the same parents and familial structure, were raised together, and grew to have similar interests and activities. They may have had similar hopes and dreams.

Memories are our perceptions of past events, experienced through our personal filters. Because they are mixed with emotions, wishes, desires, dreams, fears, and false egos, memories are often less than accurate.

Matching Memories

Although we have yet to ascertain exactly how the mind works, we do know that, in response to our life experiences, the subconscious mind makes connections and correlations between a multitude of images, feelings, sounds, smells, and other sensory data. In the process of recalling a memory, the brain searches for a match to previously stored information and then locates it. Some of that information is stored in ancient memory banks from long-ago lifetimes. A present-time event may elicit a sense of recognition that we cannot verify based on anything we remember. We may dismiss that sense of familiarity, or it may make us curious enough to investigate further.

Once your client becomes accustomed to allowing memories to surface from the deeper regions of the subconscious, it is easier for her to access more of the memories stored there. Gaining access in this way requires attention to often subtle signals and details, and the patience to systematically decipher their meaning.

The more frequently we attend to these deeper memories, the more easily they are accessed, and the more readily we recall related memories from the same incarnation. Although a person may not speak fluent French after a regression to a French lifetime, that language may start to sound more familiar and become easier for her to learn. Some of my clients have emerged from past life regressions having regained knowledge of herbs, healing, customs, skills, and other information that was previously unknown to them.

Sorting Out Memory from Fantasy

Remembering a past life does not feel the same as remembering a present life occurrence, nor does past life recall feel as though one is making up a story. During a regression, we touch on memories that seem to activate a different part of the brain than the part that is active when we create a fantasy. Even the sensory qualities of past life memory are distinct from what is experienced during storytelling.

Stop reading for a moment and think of a memory you have of this life, perhaps a childhood event. As you continue to move through that memory, notice whether any particular area of your brain seems to be especially active.

Do you feel activity at the rear or the sides of your head? With your eyes closed, make a mental image of where, spatially, you seem to be storing the information about that earlier event.

Now switch modes and concentrate on making up a story. Perhaps you will think of a story that you might tell a child at bedtime. While creating that story, once again locate the part of your brain that feels most active. Again, make a mental image of the location of that part of the brain where, spatially, you have come up with that story.

This exercise may seem a little silly. However, when you become sensitive to discerning how you feel when your memory is active, as opposed to how you feel when you are creating stories, you will more easily be able to determine whether you are experiencing true past life memories or fabricating them.

Clues to veracity: Eye movement

By watching eye movements, you, the outside observer, can help your clients determine whether they are remembering or fantasizing. To experiment with this technique on your own, enlist a friend to help you. Place two chairs directly across from one another, separated by a few feet.

Have your friend observe the movements of your eyes while you tell a story that you personally remember. It might be something that you did just that morning. Then have her watch your eye movements as you tell a fictional story from the first person perspective. Spend about five minutes each telling the memory and the fictional story, so that the observer has time to become accustomed to your personal expressions.

Your friend will probably notice a number of differences: in the frequency of blinking, whether you glance more to the right or left, or upward or downward. There may be fidgeting, a change in the brightness of your eyes, or tension in your face. There are too many observable details to describe here; however, the exercise is usually fascinating for both parties. You may learn many things about yourself and your friend as you practice.

This same exercise can be useful in determining whether or not someone is telling the truth. After all, memories are the same as truth, and fantasy will register the same as a false statement.

Intuition: True or false?

Your client may experience an intuitive "knowing" as to whether the information he has retrieved rings true. Since this is a bit tricky to trust, always encourage him to test his intuition for accuracy. Even intuition comes through our perception filters.

Remind the client not to let emotions sway him concerning the veracity of his experience. Wanting to believe the information does not necessarily confirm its accuracy.

When newly-recovered past life information is allowed to settle over a few days, a client often gains perspective on it. Continue to encourage him to be guided by his intuition to access new information, but be sure to follow up with successive regressions as well as any research that can be done to verify the experiences.

Seeking historical records

A few lucky folks are able to access information that is sufficiently lucid and detailed to allow them to check their past life memories against historical and court records, cemeteries, maps, and other hard evidence.

When regressing to past lives, always ask for the date and the name of the location. Search for details of clothing, uniforms of war, insignias, flags, coats of arms, and the names of people and streets. In other words, search for information that your client probably would not have known otherwise.

Having identified these details, you can prepare your client to investigate further. Much of the research on her memories can be done on the Internet. Court and hospital records, encyclopedias, newspapers, historical societies, and many other resources can aid her inquiry.

During a past life regression one of my clients remembered quite specifically the exact location of a tombstone, including the name and date of death. He was so determined to verify the information that he drove across the country and found the gravesite!

Another client was so lucid in her ability to acquire details during a regression that she named the street address of her home, as well as her name and the names of her husband, children, and grandchildren from that previous lifetime. Since that incarnation occurred during the 20th century, my client was able to investigate the validity of the information. She wanted to meet her past life children, who were still alive. Luckily for her, that past life had taken place only an hour's drive from her present life home.

Other ways to substantiate past life memory

When your client has exhausted her research or if she finds it impossible to do, there are a few other ways to substantiate her memories.

Ask her, "Did the details of your story surprise you?" Find out whether the client searched through her mind during the regression for answers to such questions as how many children she had or the nature of her occupation, only to be astonished by the answer that came up.

Ask, "Would you have made up that story?" Generally, the stories heard in my office during a regression are everyday life events, speckled with a little romance or adventure, but often containing elements of tragedy. Most people agree that if they were to make up a story, they would endow it with more chivalry or adventure, omit the embarrassing or shameful elements, and give it a happy ending.

Most people are not royalty or members of a privileged class, do not make a profound mark on the state of the world, and, at some point in their lives, experience emotional or physical pain. Our past life memories reflect this truth.

An emotional reaction to the information may indicate that the memories are correct. A person may cry, become frightened, laugh, or feel deep shame or regret. These emotions are not elicited from anything happening in the therapy office; they are responses to the experiences recalled in the mind of the subject.

Filtering Reality

Because we are continually inundated by massive amounts of information, our brains simplify our lives in the physical world by creating a system that selects only necessary or desired information to reach the conscious mind. These filters sort incoming information, bringing to conscious awareness only those bits that are deemed relevant.

Over the course of many lifetimes, these mental filters adjust to suit the needs of the individual, based on cultural and social norms, the will to survive, and other practicalities. These filters typically act as a means of protection and survival.

During a regression you may discover certain filters that are blocking information which you and your client want to know. This may include sensing auras and spirit guides, knowing the truth about ourselves and the natural world, remembering past lives, and even being cognizant of present life memories that have been blocked. Such filters not only prevent us from being aware of such information but also can serve to support only the data we choose to recognize.

One example of a typical filter is the difficulty we have in seeing the good in a person we detest. In the same way, we may refuse to accept negative information about people whom we love and trust. Our mental filters help us latch onto facts that support our views, while discouraging our awareness of facts that might refute them.

A college student came to see me to resolve some negative emotions she had toward her father. During our session she explained that her father had divorced her mother when my client was 11 years old. She felt certain that her father didn't love her, and that the divorce proved it. She was crushed by the event, and it had affected many areas of her life.

During our session, she regressed back to the time when she was in the womb. She moved forward in time to her present age, recalling the details of her father's affection toward her mother and herself, including his excitement about the pregnancy and birth, his involvement with her from conception to adolescence, and the emotional and financial support that he had provided to her.

By the end of the session, my client was fully aware that, due to her immaturity and confusion, she had misinterpreted the cause of the divorce. She was touched to realize that her father had loved her all along. An 11-year-old's interpretation of the events of the divorce had tainted her adult assumptions about his feelings for her.

At the end of the session, the woman was full of energy and joy. She and her father had been estranged, but she now announced that she was going to contact him directly and reestablish their relationship. Her filters, which had defined her parents' divorce as evidence of her father's ill regard, had veiled her ability to see the truth of the situation.

Examining your filters

How have your personal filters distorted your own view of reality? A major part of any spiritual quest consists of identifying your filters, adjusting or removing them, and thereby moving toward a clearer view of reality. This process of increasing objective awareness of your experience gives you an expanded perspective that often greatly alters your perceptions of the past and changes its present effect on you in beneficial ways.

When you dream, your mind takes concepts and emotions and creates objects, action, and a story line. These elements do not actually exist; rather, they are one way that your mind communicates.

When you leave the physical body by astral projection to another level of experience, there is no physical world to observe "out there." Your mind registers colors, energy, and patterns, and then translates that information into pictures, objects, and events, allowing you to decipher the experience as something meaningful.

For instance, when you see your spirit guides, they do not really exist in that particular form in the astral plane, since nothing physical exists on that plane. Your mind, however, wanting to be helpful, translates their aura and energy patterns into facial features, clothing, and physique. Such details can be projected into your mind from your guides themselves or they can be your own mental interpretations, drawn from whatever raw data is available and used to create a recognizable image.

The essentially spiritual quest to gain a core understanding of your personality and character gives you extra leverage in examining your past life memories because your perceptions of yourself in those memories—how you interpret your responses, character traits, and moral choices—are all tempered by your present-day filters. Whatever you are unwilling or unable to grasp will not typically be revealed. In such cases, valuable past life awareness and wisdom will be barred from ameliorating your limitations in this lifetime.

You will gain access to blocked information only when you are ready, meaning that your filters can shift. The simple realization that you have certain filters operating, and that they are shifting to allow you access to new information, provides encouragement along your path of self-realization. When you are capable of receiving additional information about yourself, and when you are willing to process the correlating emotions, you can take heart in the knowledge that you have grown spiritually.

As you adjust and clear your filters, you come ever closer to self-actualization and enlightenment. Only your filters stand between you and the full experience of the truth.

Modes of Experience: Visual, Auditory, and Kinesthetic

Events that have the greatest impact on our lives also have the highest probability of being recalled from our memory. When an experience involves multiple senses and is composed of intense emotional or physical stimuli, we describe it as a memory cluster. Remember a wedding, funeral, accident, or graduation. During an event of import in your life, you focused intently on the information presented to you. You are more likely to remember moments or days that carried life-changing effects than those when you were engaged in routine chores or activities that involved fewer sensory stimuli.

We have three primary modes for storing and recalling information: visual, auditory, and kinesthetic. As we guide a client through the process of regression to a past life, it is helpful to know her preferred mode(s) of experience. We can better facilitate inspiring insights for our client by remaining alert to the mode, or modes, in which she is responding and remembering during her regression experience.

Visual

People who are primarily visually oriented tend to recall their memories by describing detailed pictures, using imagistic language. Visual experiencers can easily create a picture in their mind's eye. Such people are often clairvoyant as well, and use visual language to describe their memories, saying things like:

- I *see* what you mean.

- Let's take a *look* at that.

- From my *point of view*...

Auditory

People who access memories primarily through auditory means are, as a rule, more sensitive to information they hear. Rather than storing a lot of visual detail, they are more likely to remember events in association with a piece of music or a catch phrase they heard. Auditory experiencers may learn concepts best by listening to a lecture; in communicating they tend to choose words that refer to auditory experience. They may say:

- That *sounds* good to me.
- I *hear* what you are saying.
- I know I need to *listen* to my intuition more.

Kinesthetic

Kinesthetically oriented clients are "feelers" who rely heavily on their gut instinct. They may be empathetic, have easy access to compassion, and use touch-oriented language. They may say things like:

- That story didn't *feel* right.
- I'm a little *touchy* today.
- I was *moved* by their thoughtfulness.

※

Most people have both a primary and a close secondary mode through which they take in the experiences of life, whether immediate or remembered. If a person's primary mode of experience is kinesthetic and his secondary mode is visual, during a past life regression he may first sense emotions from that former time, and only after that become able to visualize the environment and events that gave rise to those feelings.

By remaining aware that people differ in their experiential modes, you can encourage your clients to discover their own method of accessing their memories, rather than reinforcing the *expectations* about past life experience they have gained through hearsay. A person trying desperately to "see" the details of past lives will be frustrated if his naturally preferred mode of experience is kinesthetic. As counselors, we must also be wary of imposing our own preferred modalities on our clients. Look for clues in the client's language and in the type of content remembered, and adopt that language in your open-ended questions to help them go deeper and access further useful past life detail.

To determine your own modality, think of the words you typically use to communicate your experiences. Ask yourself whether you prefer to learn hands-on, by *doing* something (kinesthetic); by *hearing* an explanation of it (auditory); or by *watching* someone else do it (visual). Also notice how you remember your dreams. Are they vividly detailed? Do you remember seeing colors when you dream? Or do you tend to remember more about the *conversations* (auditory) you have with others than how they *looked* to you (visual)? Are your *emotions* (kinesthetic) while dreaming more memorable than the way things *looked* (visual) in the dream?

The more experience your client has with past life regression, the more easily his memories will flow. He may also develop stronger images or other sensations. It is as though each journey into a past life cuts a groove in the pathway between the subconscious memory bank and the conscious mind's ability to access it. Thus, each time we venture back into our pre-birth past, we feel closer and more related to that previous incarnation: it becomes real to us again.

Pay attention to all responses

During one of my early experiences of regression to a past life, I found it quite difficult to get any visual data. Because my very first experience venturing back to a past life had been so vivid and fascinating, I probably had high expectations; consequently, I may have been trying too hard. Anyway, nothing was coming for me. After a few minutes of frustration, I began to notice a growing tension, starting at my collarbone and moving down my left arm to my wrist. I thought it was peculiar so I paid attention to these physical sensations. Soon I realized that I was experiencing a past life memory in which I was aiming an arrow on a longbow. The tension was the sensation of pulling back the bowstring before letting go of the arrow. I had been so intent on *seeing something* that I almost failed to notice the kinesthetic aspect of my experience: the muscular tension. But as soon as I acknowledged my physical experience, the visuals appeared. When I recognized the image that went with that sensation in my neck and arm, the whole scene developed in my mind's eye, and then I was able to move through the past life easily.

I was a female in that lifetime, engaged in a battle with swords and bows and arrows. In the next scene I felt sad and frightened. Focusing on that emotion, I remembered I had received a message that my father was in danger.

My experience illustrates the value of paying attention to *all* physical and emotional responses during a past life session, even when the picture of the events is unclear. In this case, my preferred mode was primarily kinesthetic and secondarily visual. Therefore I was leading with memories of physical sensations, followed by the visual data that confirmed and helped me make sense of them.

So What Is Real?

How do we know if our memories or our clients' memories are true or false? What do we do with all these ideas of filters and perceptions? If we understand that most memory is simply our *perception* of what happened rather than a record of objective reality, we can relax into the experience and realize that we are receiving and processing many layers of information at once. We can learn a great deal from experiences encountered during regression sessions, whether or not the events that we perceive as past lifetimes are later found to be historically accurate.

Even if the client's memories are not representative of a past life at all, they still can offer valuable information about the individual's perception of herself and her world.

Even viewed purely as metaphor, striking correspondences typically exist between the past life story and some event or situation the person is experiencing in her present life. Perhaps she is facing a similar physical challenge, moral dilemma, or relationship issue. Considering past life information as metaphor often brings inspiration and support to the client's current life dreams and goals.

Whether you are certain that your client's regression information represents a past life or if you view it simply as a metaphor, it contains a meaningful message.

The ways that people experience past life regressions are varied. Some clients experience a regression almost like a movie, while others report catching glimpses of still pictures. Some describe a "knowing" rather than seeing inner visions. When free reign is given to the mind's creative and imaginative capacity, the experience of a regression may gain more intensity: adding color, detail, and emotion.

In fact, emotions are almost always attached to the thoughts or visions that emerge during a regression, providing a helpful indication either that the memory is valid or that it has significance to the client as a personal metaphor. An emotional reaction to a past life memory is a strong hint to go deeper in the search to understand what the client has uncovered.

Sometimes difficulty arises when a client experiencing a past life regression harbors expectations of a bold, colorful, vivid experience. In our current life on Earth, we are continuously inundated with loud noises, strong smells, brilliant colors, and other poignant sensations. During a regression, our experience is more like recalling a dream than reliving an experience.

Your client will most likely be fully aware, throughout the session, that he is present in this world, in his current life. At the same time, he will be aware of another storyline and of emotions that are not related to his present-day experience. While remaining conscious of his current lifetime, he will simultaneously be aware of information that belongs to another time and another life experience. Your client will be fully capable of speaking and narrating the story even as he is experiencing the past life as a sort of dreamlike alternative experience.

CHAPTER FIVE
Special Considerations

Remembering the Death Experience

Some people fear that if they remember severe pain or death in a past life regression, their body may re-experience the same physical symptoms, even to the extent of again causing death. Although vast numbers of people have experienced past lives, I do not know of anyone who has died in the process!

It is not dangerous to experience past life memories of painful sensations or even of death. When the past life memory involves pain, people do report discomfort, however. If this occurs, simply instruct your client to move past that event until she reaches a time when comfort was regained, and the sensations will be relieved. Remember, during a regression the client's memory is not restricted to experiences only occurring between birth and death. If the client is recalling a painful death, you may guide her past that event to the point of release from the body (and thus, release from the painful physical sensations). From the perspective of the next moment, the client will be able to access the memory of her past life counterpart and recall the painful event from a more distanced perspective.

Most regressing clients express relief, relaxation, and calm once they have experienced the death process and left the physical body. The experiences immediately preceding death are often a great deal more traumatic than the actual experience of death itself. When clients remember their deaths, none report pain once the spirit has lifted away from the physical body; just the opposite, in fact. Especially when a great deal of pain accompanied the dying process, death itself is often experienced as a great relief, as in the following excerpt.

C: It is the 1920s or '30s, during the Depression. I have a hard time breathing . . . I'm in a shaft and there is no air. There has been an explosion. It's hot, wet, dirty, and we're running out of air. They are all clawing at something. We're as good as dead already, so there's no point trying to get out.

ML: What do you know about this event?

C: We—these men and I—supported the union. They set us up. And now we're dead. I'm a man. I'll never see my family again. I have a baby, and I won't see him grow up. At last everyone settles down: they're exhausted. A candle is flickering . . . and then it all goes black.

ML: What else do you know about yourself?

C: I'm about 25 years old. I was just married. My wife asked me not to go to the meeting. But I knew my child would spend his life in poverty if we didn't do something about the situation, so I had to go. Now nobody is even talking. It's quiet. It smells like cordite, gunpowder. Those sons of bitches! Nine of us died! Not all of us were at the meeting, either; some were here just doing their shift. I feel so guilty that they got hurt. They're dead now because they were in the wrong place with the wrong people. All of us knew there was a risk. We had seen people being beaten up. The word came down the line that they were planning something big, but we didn't believe it. We shouldn't have been so damn naive.

ML: What else do you experience there?

C: It's so dark. I shouldn't have shot my mouth off. Now these guys are dying . . .

ML: If that aspect of you there could give you his wisdom, what would he tell you?

C: It's not the way to do things. It was irresponsible. It's not the way to go about a change. Offer your ideas as a gift, a possibility. Don't try to change things in big chunks all at once. It's easy to whip up a crowd. but then people get hurt. There is a better way.

ML: If you could offer him your advice, what would you tell him?

C: It wasn't his fault. His passion was great and his purpose was noble. If he knew another way to make a change, he would have done it. He left a legacy of commitment to his children. They'd know him as a courageous man. That makes it easier for them and he goes on through them. I think he feels better now; there is some joy in his heart. He was stuck on that.

ML: What have you learned from this that will help you in your life here?

C: There are all sorts of ways of doing things. I can trust my native intelligence. I don't always have to be the leader, I can be a member of the group.

As they recall the moment of death, most people describe floating, relaxing, and enjoying the sensation of being out of the physical body. Some stay around and observe the deathbed scene with loved ones gathered around. Others turn their attention rather quickly to their new environment, ready to explore and discover who and what can be found in this other realm. Some describe loved ones waiting, or spiritual guides, colors, or energy. Overall, people feel supported, loved, safe, and happy.

Occasionally someone remembering her death will report distress: most often due to regrets or unfinished business from the lifetime she is leaving. She may have died quite young, by an accident or other untimely means. In some cases, the person feels tremendous grief at leaving her young children or her mate. Most problems of this sort are alleviated when one is vigilant during the physical lifetime: keeping choices ethical, expressing feelings to loved ones, and living life to the fullest.

When my favorite uncle died, I hypnotized my cousin so he could communicate with his father. He wanted to have a final conversation to put closure on the relationship and to inquire about what should be done with all the tools his father had kept in the basement. To the great surprise of my cousin, who had never done anything like this before, my uncle appeared. My cousin found it curious that his father appeared as a young man: vital, energetic, and excited. His father really didn't care at all about what was done with the things he had left behind. My cousin said, "It's like he is tapping his foot, anxious and impatient." When we inquired about this, my uncle replied that after dying he realized there was so much more to the universe than he ever imagined, and that he was anxious to move on, explore, and have some adventures.

The two had their conversation, and then my uncle was off to enjoy his new realm. My cousin felt good about putting positive closure on their relationship and was able to disburse my uncle's material goods without remorse or guilt.

Grieving

In the process of experiencing many past lives, a person may settle thoughts and emotions about the dying process in general or about the death of a loved one.

A female client once came to me with several concerns about relationships that she felt could be resolved through past life regression. She wondered about the future of her relationship with her boyfriend, James, since the two of them didn't share the same spiritual path. My client reported a very close relationship with her mother and was experiencing intense fear that her mother might be injured or die. She was also curious about her relationship with her father, since they had never been close. As I guided her into a trance by asking her to imagine a hallway, she began to describe the door she had chosen to enter.

C: It's a white door with a silver knob. There are three separate pieces of wood in it. It is not really distinct, but the white paint is chipped and the knob is shiny.
ML: How do you feel when you stand in front of that door?
C: I'm feeling calm.
ML: As the door opens, and you move through it, what do you notice?
C: I see a tree and a swing and children playing. The swing is a piece of wood with two ropes and it's hanging from the tree. There is a girl on the swing. She has dark hair and dark eyes. She is between five and seven years old. I think that is me. I'm happy. I'm wearing a white dress.
ML: What else do you notice about this scene?
C: There is a man. Is it my father? I'm not sure, but it feels that way.
ML: What else do you notice about him?
C: He has the face of my grandpa (in this life) who died before I was born. I feel respect

for this man, and I'm not scared. I also feel the presence of a woman. She is wearing an apron. She comes out of the house. I feel no connection to her. I think that man is my grandpa from this life. That's odd, as I never think of him. I see his face and I feel respect.

ML: What else do you notice?

C: I see my mother's face. I feel the love I have for her and I cry. It makes me sad to feel how much love I have for her. But it makes me happy, too.

ML: Where do you feel that sadness in your body?

C: It's in my throat and chest.

ML: As you focus on that area of your body, what else do you know about those feelings?

C: Now it is not so much like sadness. I wanted to touch my mother, but she is gone.

ML: What do you know about the circumstances around her leaving?

C: We are outdoors. It is daytime and we are near the ocean, on the beach. We are holding hands and walking, noticing the indentations of our footprints in the sand. And then the waves cover our footprints and the sand is all smooth again. I feel a shaking in my head, and then it stops. It's the sadness. It feels like my baby is gone. Something happened.

ML: What do you know about what happened?

C: My child drowned. She was my daughter. She was two years old, and I was about 20 or 30 years old. I let go of her, and she drowned in the ocean.

ML: Go back to the beginning of that episode and tell me what you remember about the events leading up to her drowning.

C: I notice horses, a lot of them, galloping through the trees. I am watching the people riding them. Now I see the baby sitting in the sand; she is my mother in this lifetime. There is that feeling of sadness. I let it happen; I lost her. Now I just see the sun and I feel light.

ML: What have you learned from observing that lifetime?

C: I understand now why I fear losing my mother so much in this lifetime. And then there is the responsibility for the loss.

ML: Asking your subconscious to take us to another lifetime—one that will help us understand more about the other relationships in your life—where are you now? Three, two, one.

C: I'm in a field. I feel like I am about 10 years old. I'm with a really cute little boy. I see flowers, white dandelions. My hands feel hot. We're playing and he's watching me. Now my feet feel cold.

ML: Do you recognize that little boy as anyone you know in this lifetime?

C: It seems like James. We're happy and he watches me. I'm running and playing. Now he is hurt or he's gone.

ML: What do you know about that?

C: It seems like someone takes him or hurts him. There was a wagon with no top, pulled by horses. Before we were playing, and afterward I'm scared and he's gone. I'm so sad.

ML: There is a part of your subconscious mind that knows full well what happened to him. As I count from three to one, that information can be revealed to your conscious mind. Three, two, one.

C: Those people killed him. It was a battle. We were seven or eight years old. Now I see that same little boy, but he is a man now. I see us with our baby, who is wrapped up in a blanket. We have other children also. We're very happy and calm. I can feel the love. My hand twitches. It has to do with the baby.

ML: What do you know about that?
C: I see myself standing on dirt. I'm feeling old. I'm with the same man, and we have had a happy life. It feels like the man was James. I also feel the energy of my father. It is good energy, but I don't really see him. Maybe he was the baby.
ML: What do you notice next?
C: I see myself walking down that big hallway again, but it is as though I am an angel. It's airy. It doesn't seem to be light or dark, but I see lights outside the hall and images of people and faces flowing by. They feel familiar. Now I notice a valley, mountains, a river, and a lake, but no people. I feel calm, I feel like it is all right to be alone.
ML: What do you notice next?
C: I see myself outdoors, walking through a field. The field has corn that is no taller than I am. I am walking home. I go into my house and walk up the stairway. It is dark and feels mysterious. I'm scared. I hide. I am afraid of something or someone. There is a man that scares me. He seems like a bad person, and I hide behind a chair. I can see him, but not his face. I feel like a teenager.
ML: What do you know about your relationship with this man?
C: He is an intruder; at least he intrudes in my life. Actually, he lives in this house, too. It's his home, but I move freely in it. Maybe I'm a maid or something. I think that he will hurt me, maybe beat me, but I'm not sure.
ML: What do you notice next?
C: He gets old and something happens to him. My fear of him is gone. I'm still there in the house; I see myself folding clothes. It's a flowing, pretty cloth or sheet. I feel happy and young again.
ML: Do you recognize that man as anyone you have known in this lifetime?
C: I don't think so.
ML: What have you learned from observing that lifetime?
C: I hear the words, "Don't be afraid; it will go away." In this life, I have been afraid a lot . . . afraid of losing my mother. And now there's the experience of that little boy . . . I see him lying there and I feel scared.
ML: Where do you notice those scared feelings in your body?
C: In my stomach and chest.
ML: When you look into that area, what do you notice?
C: The little boy still watches me. I'm sad and he is comforting me. He gives me energy and protects me. He says that it's all right, and I understand. I also see the ocean and the little girl; she is watching me, too. She wants to be back there with me, and she feels sorry for me. She loves me and wants to help. I understand that if I lose my mom, she is not really gone. I will see her again, even in this body. She is offended that I cannot accept the thought that she would still be around after her death. I am not ready for her to be gone.

At this point in the session, I facilitate desensitization techniques that allow her to become more comfortable with the possibility of eventually losing her mother. At the end of that exercise she continues.

C: Now the possibility of my mother dying seems almost fictitious, more distant. Losing her is not so present, not here in the now. When she leaves me, I see that she comes to talk with me. She is guiding me. She is there. I know now that it is easier for her to communicate with me if I relax and feel her presence. If I make it harder, she can't get through to me.

ML: Let's visit one more lifetime that will help us to understand your relationships. What do you notice this time? Three, two, one.

C: As the door slides open, I walk through into something goopy and muddy. It is night and it is raining. I'm a girl. My little sister holds my right hand. There is a boy, too, who is about two or three years old. We also have another sister who is older, but she is not there right now. We are in the house, sitting around the table eating. There is a terrible storm outside. It begins to tear down our home. It is so dark; we are so scared. Now I see us running. We're lost and scared. We are walking through that goop. It was a tornado. Now we sit in the dark, really afraid. I don't see our parents; maybe they're dead. I am comforting my siblings.

ML: What do you notice about your connections to any of your siblings?

C: The little boy seems to be my boyfriend, James, in this lifetime. The girl is one of my girlfriends here.

ML: What else do you notice about this lifetime?

C: We were happy before the tornado, and we are happy afterward. As we get older, the three of us are still together. We live in a different house, near the river. We work together to make our lives happy. It feels inspired. We learned to overcome our hardships.

ML: How do you think knowing about this experience will help you in this lifetime?

C: I don't have to fear that bad things may happen. It will be all right. Things will work out, and we will all keep coming back together.

In the session above, it was apparent that the client's experiences from a variety of lifetimes had contributed to her generalized fear response. She also witnessed many facets of her relationship with her boyfriend through the regression. With very little therapeutic intervention, by gaining a deeper understanding of the past life roots of these emotions, she has been able to resolve her fears concerning her mother.

Resisting Life: Reconnecting with Life Purpose

I was seeing a client who had been doing a good deal of self-discovery and was ready for the next step. She reported often wanting to "get out of here." Although she insisted that she would not commit suicide, she admitted to flirting with danger at times, hoping that an accident would end her stay on Earth. In the session excerpted below, this woman intended to discover her life purpose. Armed with this information, she reasoned, she might begin to relax in her life, or at least understand why she was here.

To access information on a person's life purpose, it is preferable to regress him to the time just prior to entering this body. During that time, one's spirit, or consciousness, contemplates choices of a particular family and set of circumstances. Those choices depend on information that is vital to the client's understanding of his mission in life, and knowing this puts him in touch with his responsibility for completing his mission.

To ensure that the client has gone deeply enough into hypnotic trance, first guide him into a past life regression and then bring him up to the moment just before entering this body. In the case of this client's regression, I began with an induction and continued with a transitional visualization: having her imagine moving down an imaginary hall and then choosing a door that will lead her into the past life that will best inform her quest for her life purpose.

This subject describes her door as plain brown wood with a round brass knob. As she opens and steps through the door, she cannot determine whether she is indoors or outdoors. "Wherever I am," she says, "it's dark." She begins to notice that she is wearing many layers of clothing; she feels confined by it. She is wearing petticoats, a skirt, and an Amish style hat. She continues:

C: There is a feeling of contentment in whatever I am doing. I see now that I am inside. There is a wood stove and I'm heating water. I'm humming and waiting for the water to boil. There is a baby in the other room, crying. The baby is wearing many layers, too; she has on a big hat that looks like the sun with ruffles and a long sleeping gown. The baby is in a fancy, homemade wooden cradle. We live comfortably, for our time—I'd say we're upper middle class. We have everything we need, but we don't live in a giant castle or anything. Now I've stopped humming. The baby is crying.

ML: Then what do you notice?

C: I make my tea. Now I'm sitting on a rocker made of the same wood. There is no real kitchen. The heat for the house comes from the same place where I make food. There is a separate room for sleeping.

ML: Do you notice anything else?

C: My heart is heavy. The humming is a cover-up. It seems my husband is at war. I see an image of him carrying a big gun. He loads it himself, like the old powder guns. I worry so much about him. There is no means of communication: no television, no radio, no newspapers, and no phones. He's just gone. And I'm here taking care of the baby. I rock in the chair until I fall asleep.

ML: Move ahead in time to the next relevant experience.

C: A soldier comes to the house on a horse. I'm feeling very heavy. I'm already crying by the time I open the door. He gives me a flag. It only has, maybe, 13 stars. It's folded so I can't tell, but it doesn't have 50 stars. Oh, this must be the American Revolution. He says to me, "Your husband died forming our new country." I go to the baby. It must be a boy because I say, "You'll follow in your father's footsteps. He was a great man. You'll be a great man, too."

ML: What else do you notice about that?

C: I don't seem to be worried, just very sad.

ML: When you think of your husband, picturing him in your mind and feeling his energy, do you recognize him as anyone you have known in this lifetime?

C: (Pause) He's my dad in this life.

ML: And do you recognize the baby as anyone you know in this life?

C: (Pause) He feels like both my cousin and my daughter. Their energies are very similar.

ML: Moving ahead now to the next relevant experience in that lifetime, what do you notice next?

C: I'm in a place that is candlelit. It is big, with open windows—much different from the first place, which was dark and felt closed in. My son is now 16 or 17. I am worried about him. He is of the age to serve in the Army, and I don't want him to go. He's so easygoing and comforting to be around. He reassures me that I'll be all right, no matter where I am. It is clear to me now that he's definitely my daughter in this lifetime.

ML: What else do you notice about this?

C: I'm very worried. He is in a uniform, and going out the door. I'm left crying again.

ML: What happens next?

C: He comes home. He's a man. I don't know how much time has passed. I'm so relieved and happy to see him. I don't know my age. He moves me to another town; we travel by horse to get there. I am wearing giant skirts and I ride sidesaddle; it's very uncomfortable.

ML: What else do you notice about this?

C: He has a wife now and she's pregnant. I feel that I will die before the baby is born. The wife feels like my son in this lifetime. Oh . . . so my children were married! She's angry about me dying before the baby is born. She needs my help. I feel her hurt, even though I'm dead. It also feels as though he (my present son) brought some of that disappointment into this lifetime. I feel as if I have to make up for it. She (the daughter-in-law, then) felt that I abandoned her . . . Now I'm dead . . .

ML: What do you experience as you leave the physical body?

C: It's freeing. It's like light. As I leave, I notice the people there, and I see my indigo aura, surrounded with a rose color, leaving. I see my aura floating upward and becoming part of the universe, floating free. It's like being in a vast ocean.

ML: As you left the body, did you notice anything else?

C: I feel the emotions of my son and his wife. They are both crying. I try to send them my essence, to let them know that I'm at peace, but I can't get through to them. I want to move on rather than stay here and dwell on this. I'm part of the ocean of the universe now . . . It's really wonderful, comforting.

ML: Allow yourself to move ahead in time and space toward the 20th century, to the moments before attaching to your body in this lifetime. What do you begin to notice about that experience?

C: The water is getting rougher, as if a whirlpool is forming. I'm resistant. I want to stay holding on to the smooth water on top. My drop of water is being sucked down. I'm being told that I need this experience. The message is given in thoughts, not in words.

ML: What do you notice about being sucked down?

C: It operates like a whirlpool. There's no way out. I have no choice. Then I notice being in my mother's womb.

ML: Going back to the moments when you are experiencing the whirlpool, what else did you know about the reasons for being sucked down?

C: I am told I need the experience. I am to help lead.

ML: Lead whom, for what reason?

C: The evolutional change is hard, and the strongest souls have to lead the people through the changes. I'm strong and have to be one of them here. The changes are much more subtle than what I've been waiting for.

ML: What do you mean by that?

C: I have been waiting for something terrible to happen to the world. This message indicates that instead there will be a lot of little terrible things.

ML: What else do you know?

C: I had no choice. This is bigger than my soul. I don't know what to call it: destiny, a master soul, a universal plan? I don't know, but I couldn't resist. My soul didn't really want to be here.

ML: And you said that you noticed being in your mother's womb. Can you tell me more about what you notice there?

C: It's peaceful, warm, and cozy in there. I feel loved and wanted.

ML: What else do you know?

C: It's so warm and comforting. I don't have any negativity or resistance while in the womb. It's even safer than floating in the universe. It's contained, but comfortably contained. It's so much fun moving around. And I can move more and more. I don't want to come out.

ML: What do you notice next?

C: I see my mother in labor. She's being pushed in a gurney. I don't see my father. They give my mother drugs to put her to sleep. I'm thinking, "No, no, I don't want to leave here." I see forceps. I didn't know that I was delivered with forceps, but since my mom was drugged, she may not have known, either. I see the doctor pulling me out with a tool on my head. I'm resisting.

ML: What do you do to resist?

C: I see myself in a headstand position: not really breach but sort of digging in with my legs. I tangle the umbilical cord around my feet. When they get me out, I'm screaming. I see my father smiling, but he's looking at me through glass. The doctors and nurses hold me first, and I don't want them. I want my parents.

ML: What else do you notice?

C: I'm screaming. I recognize my father right away. I'm not sure I knew my mother from before; however, I feel safe with her, she'll take care of me. It's obvious to me that I really know him. I feel the energy connection between us. I see a color dance—our auras—and have the sense that we're back together again. It's hard to describe. I just had a flash! I saw that same colorful energy dance with both of my kids at their births. They came early; they wanted to be here.

ML: What else do you notice about your birth?

C: My mother is glowing when she wakes up and gets to hold me. The connection is still not clear, but it feels like she will be my protector.

ML: So does this experience help you to understand why you are in this life, even though you always have felt the resistance to living?

C: It answers the question, yet it doesn't make it any easier. I now know that it's bigger than I am. Now I can remember that fact when things get difficult.

This regression answered my client's questions about her reasons for coming into this life and helped her reconcile her feelings about being here. As a clinical example, it provides a valuable description of the kind of experience that may occur between lives and during the birth experience.

Which Lifetime to Experience?

The subconscious mind may be allowed to choose which lifetime to observe, or it may be directed to recall a lifetime that will inform the client about a particular subject. The subconscious is quite cooperative and will provide past life information based on whatever guidelines it is given.

A client may choose to visit a lifetime or lifetimes to learn more about her relationships with people she knows currently. If her concerns center around work or career, she may choose a lifetime in which she practiced a similar occupation or had a specific talent. She may choose to regress to the past life during which she acquired a phobia which still plagues her, or to discover the root cause of an illness. When someone faces a difficult or important decision, the subconscious mind can be directed to lead her back to a lifetime during which she faced a similar choice. Looking back into our past life history is like reading our old journals: we remember insights and life lessons that may have faded from our awareness. In this way, we regain forgotten wisdom and are able to make better life decisions in the present.

Visiting the Future

Time is not experienced in the same way in every realm of existence. There are places in the reality of space/time in which all of time exists simultaneously, and states of consciousness that can be achieved in which we may readily observe all aspects of the past, present, and future. From this perspective there are infinite versions of the future awaiting us. We may visit them; we may even choose to live in them. Or we may simply take a quick glance from where we stand and say, "No thanks!"

It is certainly possible to visit the future; however, what is revealed there may help us to choose a different outcome. For example, when someone receives information about his future in a psychic reading, he may not like what he sees. He is then free to make changes in his behavior, thoughts, and words that will effect the desired change in his future. Although the reading may have been accurate for the time in which it was given, the questioner's skillful use of his free will can prevent that future from coming to pass.

In the same way, we are able to visit our future lifetimes: a process that is termed progression rather than regression. Progressions can be informative and useful. A word of caution, however. Go far enough into the future that you do not reveal information about this current lifetime that might be harmful to yourself or to your client. For example, if your client progresses 10 years into the future and notices that she is in another body, living in another location, you can assume that her present life will be terminated in 10 years or less. That knowledge may make her behave in ways that can be harmful to her evolutionary path. This is not necessarily so, but it is wise to be aware of the risk.

Some people can handle information about the near future in a balanced way, while others will have a difficult time. Think deeply and carefully about possible ramifications before attempting progressions.

The benefit of a progression often lies in viewing the future state of world affairs and noticing how you will be dealing with them. A progression may inspire someone to gain more knowledge or to fulfill her current life purpose, so that she will be ready when the future comes. She may be motivated to become more ecologically or politically active, or to seek personal enlightenment with new vigor.

When doing a progression, always keep in mind that the future your client sees may not be the exact future that she will later experience, due to the great number of life-changing choices she will inevitably make between now and that future time.

In my early years as a regressionist, I had a client who progressed spontaneously during a session. She described the United States in the aftermath of a polar shift. She described scenes of mass destruction, flooding, loss of electricity, and many more hardships. One day some time later, I received a phone call from a colleague whom I had never met in person. During our discussion, she referred to a client of hers who had described exactly the same scenes, in the same detail. Our clients lived two states away from each other and were not acquainted.

In the 1980s I had another client who requested hypnosis in order to understand some missing time she had occasionally experienced since childhood. She went into a very deep trance and yet she was able to tell her story fluently. She saw herself on another planet being trained as a guide for humans who were to be relocated there. When asked about the year, she said it was in the early 2000s. I was silently concerned that the date indicated she would have an early death in this lifetime. When I asked in what year she had been born, however, she replied, "In the 1950s." I understood that she was progressing to a later period within her present lifetime.

The session proceeded for about an hour, revealing detailed information about her off-planet experience, her role in the relocation plans, and the experience of unexplained loss of time. In her case, apparently, her childhood imaginary friends had actually been visiting alien entities who escorted her during journeys to another planet. When she emerged from trance, she did not remember anything about the experience or what she had said to me.

Although such stories are rare, dozens of my clients, while in trance, have recounted similar abduction experiences. We do not generally seek out such memories; rather, we come across the information while exploring other subjects and issues. These experiences may be out of the ordinary, but they are not out of the question.

How Many Lifetimes?

Although it is possible to experience an infinite number of past lives, it does not mean that we have been everybody else at some point in time. To understand how an infinity may be exclusive, imagine two circles. Within the perimeter of each circle there contains an infinite number of points, as in basic geometry. Yet none of the infinite number of points in one circle are the same points as the infinite number in the second circle.

No one can be certain how many lifetimes an individual may experience over the course of his existence. Common sense would indicate that the number will be different for each individual. Not only might someone incarnate untold times on Earth, there exists the possibility that incarnation could also occur elsewhere.

We live in an infinite universe. There are few limitations, and the number of lives a person may experience is unrestricted. In this sense, we all live one big lifetime which is divided into parts, much like a big book separated into chapters. We are alive when we are in our physical bodies on earth, and we are alive when we are out of our physical bodies in the astral. Our consciousness continues through all these changes. The question, then, becomes: "How frequently do we return to the physical state?"

Other Worlds, Other Possibilities

According to the United States Geological Survey (www.usgs.gov), scientists now claim that the universe is somewhere between 11 and 15 billion years old, the Milky Way galaxy is between 11 and 13 billion years old, and Earth is about 4.5 billion years old. This information demonstrates that the number of years during which it has been possible to exist on Earth is plus or minus one-third of the years in which life forms and experiences could have existed in other places in this universe.

It is at least unimaginative and, at worst, arrogant to think that our planet, or even our galaxy, is the only one on which life forms have successfully developed. Beyond our universe there may be an infinite number of other universes defined by three or more of the 12 known dimensions; thus, there are vast numbers of places in which a soul might incarnate. For this reason, we must also consider the likelihood of souls incarnating on other planes of existence. From this perspective, the age of a soul, or the number of possible lifetimes, is fathomless.

Old Soul or New Soul?

You or your clients may have heard references to people being old souls or new souls. What does that mean? Whenever you discuss such concepts, it is wise to understand a definition. These terms can mean something different to each person.

Most people calculate their progression through life in relationship to chronological time ticking away on our own particular planet. I invite you to practice expanding your consciousness, and begin removing the limitations you've placed on your imagination and your view of the possibilities of this world. The scientists of new physics are now demonstrating that all time and space exist here and now. All moments, all aspects of reality in consciousness, exist simultaneously. According to this concept, all of our alternative lifetimes are happening right now! It also means that all of consciousness is eternally in existence.

A "new soul" is not created at a beginning in a linear path of development. When a soul individuates, it already has a set of aspects, in what we would term the past, present, and future. The more "advanced soul" cannot have had a longer existence in time. Rather, it possesses a greater density of experience, awareness, and knowledge.

Generally when I have witnessed people referring to younger and older souls, they are reflecting on the person's spiritual focus. When a person is spiritually oriented and has acquired depth of wisdom, she is labeled an old soul. On the other hand, when a person has closed down her thinking, ignored her spiritual nature, and paid little attention to her own growth and development, people refer to her as a young soul. Strong arguments could be made against this method of measurement, however, and to the way that the terms are applied. Imagine a person who has gained great wisdom and power in earlier lifetimes, and who then had an overwhelmingly traumatic experience in a more recent lifetime. She may have chosen to shut down or to reverse her path for a while out of fear or pain. She may appear to be "new" on her path when, in fact, a certain experience has simply put her on a different course.

Take a moment to reflect on your own state. How many lives do you imagine that you might have had? Were you more powerful and knowledgeable in ancient lives, or are you now expanding beyond any previous limitations? Exploring these questions can help to free us from preconceptions about our clients, as well as ourselves.

Keep in mind that when we make changes in this moment, they reverberate throughout all the aspects of that spirit, creating change on all levels—past, present, and future.

Dimensions and Awareness

Geometry teaches us that planes are defined by dimensions. The earth plane is defined by the three dimensions of length, width, and height. Calculations by mathematicians suggest there are twelve known dimensions, known by the following names: length, width, height, gravity, electricity, magnetism, weak atomic force, strong atomic force, Higg's Field, dark matter, dark energy, and time. Any combination of three or more of these can produce a plane. Any plane has the potential for creating inhabitable worlds.

Notice that each of the dimensions of our physical world is perpendicular to all others. Width is perpendicular to both height and length, while length is perpendicular to both height and width. Any other dimension will be oriented at right angles to all others, as well. This visualization is extraordinarily difficult for the three-dimensional brain to grasp; we have to struggle to perceive the nature of other dimensions.

To demonstrate, a three-dimensional cube casts a shadow on a table. That shadow is two-dimensional, having only length and width. If we could turn the shadow and observe it along its edge, *its* shadow would appear to be a one-dimensional line, having only length. If we turned that line on its end and looked down on it, it would appear to be a zero-dimensional point.

So a point is the shadow of an inverted line, a line is the shadow of an inverted plane, a plane is the shadow of an inverted cube, and a cube is the shadow of something four-dimensional. What do you imagine that four-dimensional object would look like?

Humans can sense the effects of other dimensions, yet typically we are not capable of seeing those dimensions in the same way that we can see length or width. With proper perception and practice, a person can learn to perceive other dimensions while out of the physical body (astral projected or deceased). Bringing that perception into our experience while in the body could, however, cause us to experience an extremely disoriented state. The spirit resides in all dimensions, yet while we reside in the physical state our conscious focus handles only the three familiar dimensions. It makes no sense to speak of becoming a five-dimensional being unless you plan to leave this three-dimensional physical body. To shift to another dimensionality, you would have to have a fundamental understanding of those dimensions, and you'd also need to be bold enough to shift the perceptual capabilities of your mind to encompass them.

Beings do exist who are naturally able to perceive, say, seven or eight dimensions, and any one of us may have been a being of more dimensions. Upon being born into this body, however, the mind becomes accustomed to the limitations inherent in three dimensions. But being in this limited three-dimensional body can produce an experience of discomfort, perhaps a sense of confinement. Until the greater scope of the soul is discovered, the cause of these sensations is likely to remain a mystery.

Astral Plane

The astral plane is a unique construct that surrounds and pervades all other planes of existence. The nature of the plane itself is malleable, and is subject to the perceptions of the conscious awareness of those operating there. It is at least three, and not more than ten, dimensions of perceivable space/time; however, there is nothing there that is physical as we know it. The astral plane acts as a kind of thoroughfare for traversing between various planes, as well as a location where disembodied spirits reside. When an individual astral projects or dies, her conscious awareness moves into the astral plane. If a person chooses to visit other realms or planes, she travels through the astral plane to reach them. Even when physically embodied, part of the soul (the astral body) also exists in the astral plane.

While focused in the astral plane, by astral projection or by death, the consciousness of an individual soul is embodied in its energy field, or astral body. Every human being has several layers of bodies. A brief explanation of each follows:

- Physical – The body
- Astral – Consciousness, self-awareness
- Spiritual – Raw energy
- Mental – Cognition, mind, some conceptualization
- Emotional – Reaction, assessment, can create fears, guilt, feelings
- Etheric – Imagination, electrical current
- Preternatural – Power, as the energy in a martial arts punch and when a man can lift a car in an emergency.

While alive, a soul's consciousness is manifest in all of these bodies. After death, the soul continues to exist in all except the physical body. Although there continues to be a variation of the physical body existent after death, it is considerably less dense and not typically visible to the physical eyes. During astral projection, the astral body leaves the proximity of the physical body and travels on its own for a short time. All bodies have sensory faculties, but they sense in different vibratory ranges.

On the astral plane, nothing physical exists. There are no physical bodies, houses, modes of transportation, or vegetation. There is no need for food, clothing, or jobs. Everything sensed in the astral is an energy field, perceived as different patterns and colors or as a certain direction, speed, or type of consciousness.

If a deceased relative is perceived during meditation, your consciousness will, with the assistance of your imagination, project the image of his familiar face, and you will "see" your departed loved one. What is actually happening, however, is that you are sensing his energy field, recognizing it, and recreating the image. Doing this helps the mind translate the information. When the mind can label events, objects, and people, it can more readily make sense of your perceptions, facilitating your memories of those impressions.

Concepts of Time

Physicists have recently begun to assert that all of time is occurring simultaneously. Their position is that chronological time, a manifestation of our physical brains here on Earth, is created in an effort to make sense of an otherwise overwhelming sea of simultaneous events.

Although we do not see time spatially, time is a dimension that we experience on the Earth plane. Chronological time allows us to experience the flow of events one after another, in an apparently logical order. For instance, an apple is picked before it is eaten. The flow of time provides concepts such as *before, after, now, tardy, patience, rush,* and *wait.* Time allows us to measure speed and distance. Time also gives us sanity, because it keeps us from perceiving all things happening simultaneously. Chronological time is highly beneficial.

However, time is not experienced the same everywhere; other planes of existence may experience time much differently. For instance, on the astral plane, where we go between lives, it is possible to move around in time: into the future and into the past, and then back to the present again. Time can be warped as well, making it possible to spend the equivalent of several years on the astral plane studying with your spirit guides, all in the course of a single night's sleep.

Perhaps you have heard the phrase, "All time is now." It expresses that all events in all lifetimes are happening right now. All moments are in a state of stasis, waiting for our conscious attention. Wherever we focus our spirit's attention, that is where we are. Each of us is presently focused in this aspect of our soul.

Point of Focus

With all time occurring simultaneously, a conscious being needs a primary focus. Without it we would be aware of all moments of our infinite experience simultaneously. Although all moments do coexist within the present, the ability to focus on one moment at a time provides continuity, adventure, learning, curiosity, discovery, opportunity for choice, and, ultimately, sanity.

Each part of our soul that is experiencing a lifetime is termed an aspect. All aspects of a soul exist simultaneously, while a focus is the part of the consciousness that pays attention to a particular lifetime. I am consciously aware of this present lifetime during which I am writing this book, and so my focus is with this aspect of being and this becomes my present lifetime.

The point of focus is the only place where healing and change can be initiated. It is only in *this* moment...and now *this* moment...that change can occur. Having said that, when we visit past lives, alternative aspects, or even memories of this life, we affect an alteration on them to some degree. The degree that they are affected is dependent on the intensity of the contact.

Imagine that every moment of the entire history of your soul could be captured on film. As you know, film consists of a length of contiguous freeze-frame shots. All of these frames exist simultaneously, yet when you see a movie, you observe the frames one after the other, in a predetermined order, at a speed so rapid that you do not notice that each frame is an individual, static photograph. The movement simply flows.

Likewise, all moments of your existence are in freeze-frame. All lifetimes, including all of the attendant possibilities and probabilities, are available in the present. Each frame has infinite auxiliary films that emanate from it in every dimension, providing infinite choice within the realm of its particular possibilities.

Be prepared to read, in the very near future, about the development of the concept that the consciousness is involved in something even more radical. It is being demonstrated that it continuously bounces, like a pinball, between vast numbers of "places", during the infinitely short intervals between those above described freeze-frames. This concept will give rise to explanations of why obscure thoughts pop into our minds, or why we may get distracted at odd moments. We can also experience moments of other lifetimes during those intervals. An interesting meditation involves the attempt to pay attention to what can be observed during those "bounces."

When considering this concept, we must also consider the possibility that you do not have to incarnate chronologically. The next time that you incarnate, you may choose to focus on a lifetime that occurred chronologically earlier than your present lifetime. Likewise, you could repeat any given lifetime. If you chose to do so; you might return to a lifetime and attempt to do things differently. Could this be one of several possible explanations for the phenomenon of déjà vu?

The concept of reliving past lifetimes gives rise to questions about what other souls living in those lifetimes would experience if you relived, and changed, your part. If your spirit repeated a lifetime, bringing with it altered knowledge and making new choices, it would not follow the exact film sequence that it followed previously. You would now be moving on one of the infinite alternative paths, in which the other people from that time were also making different choices or having different reactions to your personality. Along this new path, there may be new people to have relationships with, and you might or might not meet with others who were present in that life previously. Making such changes would necessarily alter the path in significant ways.

Scientists are now beginning to suggest there is no beginning or ending of time. Contemplating this concept provides another fascinating meditation.

True Success

Each of us is already successful. The conditions of our lives demonstrate, at any given moment, the sum total of all choices we have ever made. In other words, our choices have led us to this present state. If the conditions of life are not working out for us, the most important question we must ask is: "What must I do to achieve a different result?" There is no reason to blame anyone or anything else. Taking responsibility for one's own life and performing proper actions is the quickest way to obtain one's goals, achieve spiritual growth, and to experience heaven on earth and beyond.

Was Everyone Famous?

Contrary to the suspicion that everyone remembers being Napoleon or Joan of Arc, the vast majority of memories drawn from past life regressions involve mundane life experiences. Once in a while someone remembers an extraordinary feat, but most past life memories are of a personal nature. Rarely do people remember experiences during which they had a major historical impact.

That said, famous people reincarnate, too. Presidents, rock stars, martyrs, and heroes all have the opportunity to reincarnate and to continue their soul's journey. If your client recalls events from the lifetime of a well-known personality, it is wise to be extra diligent in your inquiries in order to discern between memory and make-believe. In the realm of the subconscious, many factors can contribute to confusion. For example, it is not unusual for a person to shift from reporting actual memories of a past life to reporting scenes from a recent movie or book. It is also easy to assume that simply because images of a certain event arise the subject lived at the epicenter of that situation, when this may not have been the case at all.

Imagine that you once lived as Napoleon's personal aide. You understood the details of the battle strategies and were intimately familiar with the daily rhythms and personal habits of this leader. Perhaps you were a bit envious of your superior and even fantasized about becoming him. During a regression to that period, when remembering your understanding of Napoleon's emotions, his relationships, and the reasoning behind his decisions, it would be easy to assume that you yourself were Napoleon. Only upon further investigation and the application of honest objectivity would the true state of affairs become clear. In such regressions, it may take diligence to discern whether you were living as the spirit of the well-known person or of someone closely related to them. As an exercise, ask yourself this question: In your present life, is there anyone with whom you identify so closely that you might believe you were that person, if you later regressed to this lifetime from a future one?

Your spirit carries with it many patterns, as it moves from one incarnation to another. If a spirit gravitates toward a leadership role or tends to be in the spotlight, she will typically continue to make decisions that foster such opportunities. When a spirit prefers being a helper, affecting the world from behind the scenes, she typically will reincarnate into lifetimes where she plays supportive roles rather than assuming positions of leadership. Some souls are attracted to roles of saintly virtue, while others may cycle through role after role of a darker nature.

As an exercise, imagine what role Albert Einstein might choose for his next incarnation. Do you envision him as a movie star, teacher, mother, assembly line worker, criminal, musician, or farmer? Does it seem likely that he would be very bright, have difficulty in school, or both? What do you know about his character that leads to your conclusions?

When examining your own energy, preferences, and comfort zones, ask yourself whether it would be natural for you to incarnate as a leader who commands the spotlight and takes big risks or as someone who does her work in the shadows, behind the scenes, or as a helper? Although you may adopt multiple roles for a wide range of life experiences, and you may switch from leadership to supporter from lifetime to lifetime, your soul will maintain certain tendencies and characteristics.

ML: What do you notice?
C: The door is a blue covered wood with a gold handle.
ML: As the door opens and you move through, what do you notice?
C: It is Roman scenery. It actually looks like a scene from the movie *The Gladiator*. Do you think I might be just making this up?
ML: Allow yourself to make it up for now. Let's see where it goes. If you were there, would you be a man or a woman, and how old would you be?
C: I would be a man, and I would be in my late 20s or early 30s.
ML: What do you see yourself doing?
C: I see myself on a chariot, going through a parade. I am standing, waving to the crowd. There are lots of people; the women are throwing flowers at me. This has been a military victory. I smile and I laugh, but I have a cut on my right shoulder.
ML: What do you remember about how that got there?
C: While I was fighting one person, another came from the side and cut me with his sword. I was in such a rage from the cut that I took my sword and chopped the head off the man that I was fighting, and in the same motion I took out the guy who cut me. Then I just went on to look for the next person to fight.
ML: What do you notice next?
C: I am in an open field. It is all cleared out. Now it is a field of people: bodies are everywhere. I'm standing at the side, looking at the bodies and at the smoke rising. I'm thinking, "Another day at work. I've accomplished my mission. It's time to go home."
ML: Where is home? And what do you know about it?

C: My home is in Rome. I have an apartment or a house on a hill. I'm single and the house is empty. But I know that I don't ever really go home, it's just on to the next battle. I have a pet tiger and a lion. I have had the tiger since its birth. It is fairly tame. I can remember picking him up as a cub and putting him on my shoulders.

ML: What else do you remember about your home?'

C: The walls are white in a Grecian style. There are vases, and gold and silver ornaments. I see a fireplace. There are marble floors. There are French doors that kick out onto a veranda. I have an Egyptian servant or two. I see a picture of the Emperor.

ML: Some time passes by and what do you notice next?

ML: I have to walk up a hill to get there. At the bottom, in the lowlands, is the main town. It is dusty and there are street vendors; I notice a snake charmer. There is a one-legged person selling fruit and children scamper around. It's not the cleanest town. I have another battle to face, which will be in a place with green trees. It feels like this will be my last battle. I'm so tired of fighting.

ML: When it is time to go into battle, what do you notice?

C: I don't want to get involved. I direct the battle more than anything else. It is a creepy fight. The enemy is barbaric and they play by different rules. I see a monkey and I look at him for answers. He indicates whether it is smart to move or to stay put.

ML: How does he communicate that to you?

C: With a smile or a chuckle. If he isn't afraid, he smiles. When he shows fear, his eyes bulge, he scratches himself, and he becomes quiet. We are successful in this battle, it was not as difficult as we had thought. The enemy was stumped. We killed a lot of them right off the bat, and the rest we took as prisoners.

ML: What happens next?

C: I leave Rome. I go to Greece. I am standing by icy blue water. I am sitting on a ledge, looking at my sandals. In the water's reflection, two angels appear. They don't say much, but tell me my work is done, it is time to move on. Now I am going through a tunnel: this may be the end. I look back at my life. They tell me, "You were not responsible for what you did." My job was to kill; I was following my orders. It is possible that I did die in that battle.

ML: At the end of that battle what do you notice happening?

C: I have a spear through my stomach as I lay on the ground.

ML: What do you notice about that experience?

C: There was a woman that I left behind. She is wearing a white dress. She has beautiful eyes and long dark brown hair. She is not my wife; she is my girlfriend.

ML: What did you learn from experiencing that lifetime?

C: Despite the killing, nothing changed. There was always just another battle.

ML: Do you recognize any correlations between that lifetime and this one?

C: I have to make sure that I make the most of what I have. The military role is just like a corporate role. You are just a tool for the corporation: you aren't really pursuing what you want to pursue. The pleasure that you receive—like a smile—can be simple. I see peasants on their knees, thanking me. They are glowing. I feel bad that they worship me, I feel as though I don't deserve it.

ML: Is there anything else that you notice?

C: There is a statue of me in the middle of town. It is white marble. In the statue, I am standing straight. I am covered with big armor.

ML: Can you read the inscription?

C: Augustus Serenus. Pompeii. XVII

ML: Moving on to yet another lifetime, as I count from three to one, the scene will open before you. Three, two, one. Where do you find yourself?

C: I'm going back and forth between two images. In the one I'm in a suit, like something Dick Tracy would wear, and I have a slick hat. I'm tall and thin. In the other I'm an old Jewish jeweler in an old three-piece suit. I hold a pocket watch in my hand and wear horn-rimmed glasses.

ML: Let's start by going into the life of the jeweler. What do you know about him?

C: It's the 1920s and I'm in New York. It is the typical old street scene in New York. There are row houses with stores along the bottom and there are buggies in the street. It's crowded. A creaky door leads to my shop. I carry high-end jewelry. The people are well-dressed. There is a fresh loaf of bread on the counter. I have a female assistant who is meek and quiet; she is dressed like a pilgrim, in old clothes.

ML: What happens next?

C: There is an explosion. The window breaks but it doesn't knock down the building. There are guys, who look like they are in a mob, snickering at me. They are trying to intimidate me. It doesn't work. I walk through the street market and someone stabs me in my side. I go to the hospital. I see myself in bed laughing and smiling. There is only one person, my assistant, who comes to see me. She rarely speaks, but she is loyal and I count on her.

ML: What do you notice next?

C: I see myself dying. It is no big deal. Then I see myself back on the street and life continues, except that my assistant now owns the shop and runs it. I'm looking in. I'm dead, yet I'm proud. She is doing a good job.

ML: What did you learn from that lifetime?

C: It felt good to leave her the shop. I passed on something valuable. It is the art of giving. It felt good to see that her long years of dedication paid off for her. Eventually she met someone, got married, and had two young boys. Now I can see myself looking down from the ceiling at those same five mob guys. I'm snickering at them because what they did was fruitless.

ML: What do you notice next?

C: I go up an elevator shaft into the clouds. Now I see a grassy field. I am back with the blond girl from the Roman lifetime. She shows me that she is always there. She is smiling. I look at the field and think, how pretty.

ML: Moving on to the next lifetime, what do you see next?

C: I see alligators. It is a jungle scene and I am a Tarzan-like adventurer. I'm in a canoe, looking at the eyes of the crocodiles. I have hired the help of some natives. I notice monkeys in the background. The mosquitoes whiz by. There are vines and humidity and big gorillas. I see a tribe now, with ornaments hanging from their noses. I'm not scared. Since being a Roman soldier, nothing can be as rough as what I've faced before—it's not a big deal. We hit the shore and I greet them. I show the leader due respect; I make him laugh and he feels comfortable. He lets us stay there. We have our own tents and nets.

ML: Move ahead to the next significant event that occurs there. What do you notice?

C: I meet a beautiful English woman. I am in my middle age years, blonde, with receding hair. I believe I am German.

ML: What are you doing there?

C: We are there to observe. We make notes and study, and we develop a deep respect for the people and nature. The woman eventually dies of a disease. After that, we leave. I see the same alligators as we leave. I sense a deep sorrow in the entire group concerning the death of that woman. The tribe was affected too.

We followed this session with discussions of his present life adventures. He continues to seek out intense life experiences.

Can You Be Your Own Ancestor?

It is impossible to determine how frequently a person may incarnate as his own descendant. In my own practice, however, I have encountered clients who remembered being part of their own family trees, for example, their own great-grandmother. Clients have also reported a deceased grandparent or another ancestor reincarnating as one of their own children in their present lifetime. Reincarnating into the same family is unnecessary, in any case, because the history and evolution of the soul, including the past life lineage, generally has little or nothing to do with one's genetic heritage or family ancestry.

During a typical past life regression session, once the client has experienced the events of a past lifetime, I request that he move to the end of his life in order to understand the conditions that existed at the termination of that lifetime. When the client has determined the age at which he died, as well as the cause of death, he releases from the body and experiences the death process itself. Even in this process, there are choices available, as we will explore in the next chapter.

CHAPTER SIX
Stepping In and Stepping Out

An interesting phenomenon may occur during regression that can make the exploration of past lives confusing. Sometimes a person experiencing a past life discovers that one lifetime began before another one ended. What are we to make of this?

One explanation is that the client is mistaken about the time period during which the lifetimes occurred: a simple error. Another possibility is that the client did not remain in the body to complete the prior lifetime. Alternatively, the person may have completed that lifetime and then stepped into another lifetime at a point midway through its lifecycle.

The term *step-in* refers to a soul who enters a body in the midst of its life. Rather than being born into a life, the soul enters a physical life through a body that is already maturing. The term *walk-in* has been used interchangeably in this context as well, though in some cases this latter term has other implications.

Two alternatives have been postulated regarding the situation of a step-in. Either the soul steps into a body whose life is already in progress, or the soul steps out of his body before it dies, allowing another soul to step in and take his place. This is a confounding concept for many people. Explanations of this phenomenon are often met with disbelief or fear. As clients acquire a deeper understanding of the process, however, it proves neither unbelievable nor scary.

Mutual Agreements Between Souls

The concept of step-ins can be alarming if you envision a spirit waltzing up and snatching your body away without your permission. On the contrary, however, in a step-in situation both parties agree to the arrangement. At a subconscious level they have determined that making this exchange will benefit the evolution of both souls.

Let's say that one person decided, at the subconscious level, that he had already completed what he came into this body to accomplish. His present mission was finished and it was time to exit so he could get into position to enter a new body and complete a task in another time and location. This person may choose to contract a fatal illness, to become involved in a fatal accident, to be the victim of a fatal crime, or come to some other physical end. On the other hand, he may choose to leave the physical body intact by allowing another spirit to enter it and take over its operation. The incoming spirit would have decided that the person's situation, personality, lifestyle, and location are all factors that would suit the accomplishment of the purpose he is seeking to fulfill.

Such an exchange may happen during a close call accident, a fright of some sort, an operation involving anesthesia, a fainting spell, or during sleep. Additionally, there have been reports of this phenomenon occurring while the person is consciously aware.

To complete the transfer, two spirits—the departing one and the incoming one—agree to the arrangement. This is always done as a mutually beneficial pact. As the departing spirit exits, the incoming spirit slides in and anchors itself in the body. Frequently, the two spirits take turns in the body for awhile before making the final switch, to acclimate themselves to the change.

People seldom remember the event of stepping in; however, in one case a female friend (we will call her Susie) recalls her experience quite vividly. Susie is a highly intuitive woman, a musician, who clearly remembers that moment in her life. She calls the spirit who left the body *Susan*.

In Susie's words, "Susan had been having some health problems, and her condition was weakening. One night while she was on stage singing with the band, she collapsed. At that moment, I clearly remember sliding down into Susan's body, while she was slowly moving up and out. We engaged each other's attention and exchanged a type of energetic embrace as we moved past each other. It is the most beautiful moment in my memory."

Susie remembers her pre-exchange conversation with the departing spirit, including the agreement to make the switch. After the exchange, she was bedridden for three days, healing the body and recovering her strength. The incoming spirit, Susie, is also musically talented and continues the singing career.

It is rare, however, that a person consciously retains the memory of this transition. Most people remain oblivious to the change. The process of stepping in is not a common occurrence; however, it is an option that souls utilize from time to time. For this to occur, one soul must be willing to leave and must be able to locate another soul willing to enter the body.

What Happens to the One Who Leaves?

The spirit that has departed the body is now free to explore the astral for awhile, to become a spirit guide if it is prepared to do so, to take a rest, to learn something new, or to locate another body, into which it can either enter or be born.

When a person suspects or confirms that she is a step-in, she tends to worry that somehow, something has happened to her. She feels some attachment to the spirit that has left. This is due to confusion about the issue. Once the person begins to understand that she herself is not the one that left, but rather the one that entered the body, she begins to relax about what happened.

This issue should not cause alarm. If it has happened to you, then you are the one that stepped in. You have chosen to enter this body and experience the remainder of this lifetime. The spirit that vacated the body has chosen to move on. He is carrying on with his own purpose, simply in a new location.

I was working with a client who discovered that he had been a musician in his previous life. He witnessed himself walking out of his manager's office at the end of a concert and simply floating out of his body, still observing the scene below. He did not remember returning to that body, although he observed his body continuing to walk to his vehicle.

In the next scene that he recalled, he was about 12 years old in the present-life body, sitting on his bed playing a guitar. He looked around and remembered thinking, "Oh, here I am." Curious and relaxed, the 12-year-old went back to playing the guitar.

After the hypnosis session, the client remarked that before that age, playing the guitar had been a struggle; he didn't play well. From that day forward, however he simply began playing with ease and talent. At the time of our session this man was working as a musician, played in a band, and had produced several CDs of his own music.

This man had never heard of the concept of step-ins, and this session was his first past life regression. Being a step-in not only explained the sudden appearance of his musical talent, but also his lack of connection to his early childhood. This episode would also explain any overlap of chronological time between the past life he remembered and his present one.

Why Step Out?

People generally choose to step out of their bodies in order to position themselves to best fulfill their goals for their next incarnation. Someone may step out to get away from a disagreeable situation or to move toward a more favorable one. These reasons may include leaving an abusive relationship or extracting oneself from a situation that is boring or meaningless in light of the spirit's aspirations. Stepping out may also accomplish a move closer to a soul group or a soul mate. The spirit may be attracted to another space or time, where it can learn new and different lessons; this may draw it away from its present incarnation.

In the mid 1980s, I was engaged in intense spiritual study and was the proprietress of a metaphysical bookstore. At that time a young lady came to spend the summer with me. During her stay, she developed second sight, learned many things about the spiritual world, and experienced a number of past life regressions. She shared her memories with me, and we discovered that we had shared many lifetimes.

She later had to move away, yet her spirit frequently visited me. It soon became apparent that she was no longer in the body of my friend. Disappointed to be living so far away from our group, she had stepped out.

A few months later, a woman in her 30s contacted me, stating that she had been interested in meeting me and now felt compelled to do so. After several contacts with this woman, it became obvious that the spirit of my young friend was now residing in this new friend. We experimented with past lives, and the woman was able to recall the same lifetimes as my previous friend; she even remembered some of the same events that had been reported in our sessions together. A few months later, this woman's husband was transferred to another state, so she also relocated. It wasn't long before the spirit in question came calling again.

After a few more months, this same spirit stepped into another young lady in her late 20s. Again, she was able to recall some of the same lifetimes. This woman was not as open psychically, so the spirit was not able to fully express itself through this body. In frustration, she eventually stepped out of that body as well. Her intent was to be near our soul group—studying, interacting, and staying focused on spiritual development.

Within another year, a close friend of mine became pregnant. The same spirit made it known that she wanted to be that child. This time she was born into a body that would keep her close by, and to parents who would foster her spiritual growth.

It is fascinating to glimpse the journey of spirits through their manifestations in the physical world. This story demonstrates the case of a spirit whose purpose of learning and being in the proximity of a certain group of people was far more important to her than remaining in a specific body.

Why Step In?

Spirits step in to more readily accomplish a life purpose or learn an important life lesson. The soul may have a need to be near a particular person, to experience a physical life while avoiding the phase of early childhood, or to live within a situation already created by another soul.

For example, three people in the present life remembered parts of the same spirit exchange that had taken place in a past life. Through regression, I remembered being a daughter of royal blood in Spain during the time of the Inquisition. The atmosphere was tense; people all around me were being tortured and killed. I believed that I was at great risk, especially because I had made a dangerous alliance with a foreign freedom fighter who had invited me to escape from the country with him.

A male friend of mine in the present lifetime, independently remembered being the cavalier man who had fallen in love with my past life counterpart. He recalled that there was something odd about my energy in the final months of our lives, but was so determined to be with me that he overlooked the changes that had occurred. On the day that the two lovers were to meet and escape the persecution of the Church, the Inquisitors located the young woman and killed her. The man waited in their secret meeting place until he, too, met his demise.

A second present-day woman remembered the end of my previous life, because she herself experienced it. Dismayed at the cruelty that was running rampant throughout the country, my spirit chose to escape by leaving that body several months before its untimely death. The second woman had not experienced a physical body on the earth plane for some time. She wanted to fully immerse herself in the harsh reality of the religious wars to gain an important lesson that would provide a lasting impression on her consciousness.

All three of us witnessed and confirmed the soul exchange of that distant lifetime through independent past life regressions.

Who Keeps the Personality?

Although your personality is considerably shaped by your spirit's memories and experiences, an imprint of it is left within the physical brain. When a step-in transition occurs, most everything that has been logged into the brain remains with the physical body. In this way, the person continues to remember childhood events and familiar people and places. In typical interactions, little will appear to have changed; however, certain habits, quirks, and interests belonging to the new spirit will begin to show through.

If the personality of the incoming spirit is stronger and more dynamic than the previous personality, the change will appear more striking to others after the transition. The person may pick up new habits or drop longstanding ones that are distasteful to the incoming spirit. He may decide to leave a long-term relationship, which makes sense considering that it was not actually his relationship to begin with. On the other hand, the new spirit sometimes steps in specifically to experience the qualities of the existing relationship.

If the outgoing personality, which has been imprinted on the physical brain, is the stronger of the two, the new spirit's personality may not show through as clearly. If the new spirit is recessive in this way, he may not be able to fully realize his intended purpose. It may prove too difficult to overcome the old personality and redirect the outgoing person's path toward the incoming personality's goals and desires. Such an inability to manage the personality can cause substantial subconscious frustration. In this case, the soul that has stepped in may choose to complete that lifetime, or he may arrange to step out again in search of a more suitable situation.

An Uncommon Experience

Although I have recounted a number of instances of step-ins here, the phenomenon is not as common as it may seem. I address it here because it does occur, and because it is, therefore, advantageous for any student or practitioner of past life regression to be aware that she may encounter the phenomenon in session.

If you understand stepping in, you will be less surprised when your client reports an overlap in time between two lifetimes. Unfortunately, the validity of past life memories has sometimes been questioned when the dates of one memory coincide with another remembered lifetime. It is wise to carefully examine and research any information recalled; however, we don't want to dismiss accurate information simply due to limited knowledge of the vast possibilities that exist in this universe.

The prospect of stepping in is not to be feared. In fact, it provides the soul with additional freedom and choice. A body is not taken by force; rather, it is exchanged for an experience more conducive to the goals and desires of the soul.

I knew two young women whose souls were so closely linked that they chose to exchange bodies from time to time throughout their early lives. Interestingly, their lives were similar in that they both had one younger sibling and divorced parents. They also both had stepmothers who were abusive. They shared a similar hair texture, as well as the same height and body type. Their interests were the same, and they both received the same gift from their fathers for their high school graduation. Neither the young women nor their families ever met face-to-face in this physical life, yet the two socialized with the same circle of friends at different times in their lives. Every few years or so, they would exchange positions and try out the other body.

This information was revealed through trance work with one of the young women, who was able to recall experiences that she had had while residing in the body of her counterpart. This client is now deceased, but the information revealed in her sessions was later verified by members of the social circle who knew them both.

Stepping In Versus Possession

Stepping in, an exchange made between two willing parties, is quite different from the phenomenon of spirit possession. The step-in arrangement helps both souls to facilitate the fulfillment of their purposes, and leaves only one spirit remaining in the body. When someone is possessed by a disincarnate being, it is generally not done with his conscious agreement. Rather, both spirits reside in the body simultaneously, which typically sabotages the life of the host. Below is part of a session during which a client discovered that she had experienced stepping in.

C: Light. Bright sunlight. I have overwhelming joy (tears). It's a really nice spot to be. It's like being free, a free spirit. I don't see anyone, but I feel connection. I believe that I am between lives. I am downloading my experiences and also getting information back, too. Fast forward. I am almost connecting with . . . there is an exchange of experiences and ideas. I feel light, airy. I am told it is time to go now. I am excited, curious, and interested. I want to learn. Now I am watching a big screen. They are suggesting . . . No, I'm being encouraged to go to Japan. I will not start as a child. Is that possible?

ML: Yes. We call that stepping in. What do you notice about that experience?

C: I will be a female. I will be 23 when I enter the body. I will be a wife with no children. My life will be my husband. I will be submissive. I see it as if on a screen, and I'm not thrilled about going there. I am told that I need to learn how to fight for, and overcome, being dominated and submissive. That sense of duty. Oh, my feet hurt.

ML: Can you tell me why your feet hurt?

C: Yes. I am there now. My feet are bound. I am not happy about being there. As I go about my chores and duties I have to learn how to . . . It is the simple things. There is a rhythm of repetitiveness, of doing dishes and how to get through that on a daily basis. It becomes meditative, almost spiritual. They are mundane tasks that I had hated. Now I take pride and strength from that whole day-to-day pattern. I look at things differently. Now I am not doing dishes. I have turned it into something way beyond that, into what I want it to be.

ML: What else do you experience or learn in that lifetime?

C: I notice a woman that I greatly admire. I knew of her and then went to hear her speak. She is strong, yet Japanese. She considers herself to be equal to all. Just because she is female doesn't make her less, or lower. She is not afraid to speak out, and she does it so eloquently. She gently nudges society slowly in her direction. She has gained their confidence and respect.

ML: How has she influenced you in that lifetime?

C: She gave me courage. I started painting. I looked within and listened to myself. I learned that I could be myself and still be responsible to my other roles. As a female in that culture I did not have much status and was not listened to.
ML: Do you recognize that woman as anyone you know in this lifetime?
C: She is my friend.
ML: How will that lifetime influence you in this lifetime?
C: I will find joy in the simple, mundane tasks and be in the moment. Life doesn't have to be complicated. Instead of looking at dishes and laundry as a pain, I can see them as a gift. I have three people in my life, as part of my journey, to help guide and care for. I don't have to be negative about my responsibilities if I approach them from a different angle. I will take delight in the simple things. I will appreciate and observe.

This woman's experience of stepping in aptly illustrates how focused and specific a spirit's reasons may be for making the switch. She needed to accomplish overcoming a certain passivity and lack of self-expression, and entering this woman's lifetime accomplished that quite adequately and in a relatively brief time.

CHAPTER SEVEN
Life Between Lives

In one of his humorous and insightful books, Douglas Adams writes, "He hoped and prayed that there wasn't an afterlife. Then he realized there was a contradiction involved here and merely hoped that there wasn't an afterlife."

Observing past lives will give us greater clarity about the birth process, the choices we make about our births, and children's awareness, even in the earliest stages of life. In cases involving pre-birth and early childhood memories, it is notable how much awareness and clarity of knowledge the embryo, baby, and child have, in regard to the environment, the people, and the emotions of everyone involved. By employing techniques for accessing past life memories, useful information regarding people's objectives for choosing a particular body and set of parents has often emerged.

The repeated visitation to past lives and the times between lifetimes provides a vast amount of information concerning death and dying. Such information can be very comforting to us as we approach these issues, both in our own lives and with our loved ones.

While experiencing a past life, a client described being in her mother's womb while the mother was walking on the beach. It was time to be born, and her mother, a member of a primitive culture, squatted on the beach and gave birth. My client remembered the entire process of being birthed: the acknowledgment that it was time to move out of the womb, the journey through the birth canal, and then being thrust out into the air, on the beach. As a baby my client claimed that one of her greatest disappointments was the lack of information. She craved instruction and understanding about her new world, even as an infant. She cried frequently, not from hunger or pain but from frustration that her vast consciousness was not being filled with useful knowledge about this fascinating world she had entered.

During a typical past life regression session, after the client has experienced the events of a past lifetime, I request that she move to the time of death to understand the conditions at that time. When she has determined the age at which she died and the cause of death, she releases from the body and experiences the death process itself.

After experiencing the death process, she'll explore what happens between lives.

Perception Alters Experience

The way we as individuals put together our reality filters plays a big part in shaping the way we view and experience reality. This same process occurs in the astral. There, too, we typically seek out confirmation of our beliefs. Christians may report seeing Jesus and speaking with him, while a Buddhist may describe passing through the Bardos (the levels of experience encountered during the death process). What you believe will color the way you define your experiences.

Remember that there is nothing physical in the astral. Your client's visual experience will actually be energy in patterns and colors. This energy may be part of a conscious being, or it might simply emanate from something or someone. The mind seeks to define this energy and its movement in terms that help us describe and explain our experience. This, in turn, facilitates our ability to remember it.

When it is sensed that a male energy has come to guide your client, he may choose to label that energy Jesus, Mohammad, father, brother, or friend. This is the client's interpretation. It may be accurate or it may not be accurate. The more you encourage your client to learn about his inner experience, the better he will become at deciphering reality, and the more accurate will be his interpretations of his experiences.

Just because you're dead doesn't mean you're smart

After witnessing numerous death experiences and observing the time between lifetimes, it will become clear that you are not suddenly enlightened merely by virtue of the death process. You do not become instantaneously omniscient. In fact, you gain only a slightly broader perspective of reality and your place in it. You may understand more about your personal cycles, the consequences of your choices, and the grander patterns of your personality and behavior, but you do not suddenly gain a body of wisdom or knowledge that was not part of your consciousness before death. After death, psychic vision is only slightly clearer.

This is an important fact to grasp and to communicate to clients, since many people think that they have only to die to escape their present dilemma or to experience complete enlightenment. They are certain they would never make the same mistakes again. People also mistakenly assume that because their spirit guide is in the astral, he or she is omniscient and has perfect vision and wisdom. In truth, it doesn't work that way at all.

If all it took was death to gain enlightenment, why aren't we all enlightened? Have we not all died and been reincarnated? If it were that easy, we all would have gained full enlightenment already. There would be no more crime, no lessons to learn, and only perfect souls remaining. For this reason, I stress to clients the great importance of gaining knowledge and broader perspectives, clarifying vision, strengthening morals, healing emotional baggage, and acquiring wisdom during this lifetime in a physical body. This world is the proving ground. It is through experiences in the physical world that we make progress.

So What Does Happen?

People who have not been practicing their sight or their ability to astral project typically will find themselves somewhat disoriented in the ways of the astral. There will be a period of adjustment, which may be brief or lengthy depending on the flexibility of the spirit's awareness and the amount of guidance she is receiving.

Sometimes, in rare cases, post-mortem amnesia occurs. The consciousness, for reasons not fully understood, may forget its most recent lifetime and be unaware that it even occurred. In these cases, the consciousness of the spirit may interpret its visit to a loved one to be taking place in a different era, most likely in a past life when they shared a relationship.

The experience of remembering death during a regression is frequently accompanied by a calm, detached, floating feeling. Your client may express delight to be free from the body, especially if she was experiencing a great deal of pain or a debilitating disease just before death.

Some people describe gravitating toward a bright light. Others describe seeing spirit guides or loved ones who have preceded them in death, or they may find themselves in a classroom learning something new. Most people are content with these sensations, often preferring this state to being in the physical body. Rarely do they regret dying or dislike the experience. When there is regret, it typically concerns a purpose that was unfulfilled, premature separation from loved ones (especially small children), or suicide.

From the perspective granted by the afterlife, my clients often come to realize that the limiting beliefs they felt bound by during their time on earth were not as devastating or insurmountable as they appeared. Once out of the confines of the body, we see the many options and alternative measures that could have been taken to improve a situation or fulfill our purpose on earth.

Since there is nothing physical in the astral, you experience only energy—in forms, patterns, and colors. For this reason, clients may report that things appear to float through them, or that they themselves seem to float through things.

The mind translates our experiences into recognizable events and identifies people, much as it did during life. We will know some of these people and some we won't know. There will be some people we want to get to know and some whom we feel are best left alone.

All communication between lives is telepathic, since a spirit, or energy form, has thoughts but has no organs for speaking or hearing.

During the between-lives phase, we eventually have to make a decision about the next incarnation. For some people, this will happen only after a long period of rest or adventure. For others, the decision-making process will occur rather rapidly. When exactly we make the decision to reincarnate may depend on what can be accomplished while out of a physical body. A spirit can use this time to explore, learn, rebalance, and make plans for the next incarnation. A spirit may even serve as a guide for a loved one.

C: I am very old. I am lying in bed, in a thatched hut. I can't get up and do much. Sometimes people come and talk to me. I spend time looking at the ceiling and thinking about life, and the beginnings and endings of things. I think about those I love and how their lives will be. I think about life, and what I know and don't know. I think about what it might be like after I die.

ML: Go ahead and release from that physical body. What do you notice as you experience the death?

C: It is kind of nice. I just slid out, calmly. I was ready to go forward after I said goodbye. I was met by someone who came to escort me. I go upward and diagonally as I leave; it feels funny. The feeling isn't tingly, but a little bit cold. It feels kind of good, but I'm kind of nervous. I'm somewhere I haven't been in a while. I'm not sure what to expect.

ML: What do you notice next?

C: I arrive, and there is someone there. He seems very familiar. He greets me with a big smile and a hug. He is proud of me. I still have the feeling of the previous body on me. He escorts me to a different place, like the courtyard of a temple. There is an altar, in a circle. We walk together the length of the garden, and he holds my arm. It is a big garden with big stones, and there are arches over the pathway. We walk up a couple of steps and stand in a circle. A light comes down like I'm taking a shower. Parts of me from before are being washed away. It is nice to be there. I feel refreshed. It is a familiar place. When we are done with that, it's like after a shower when you put a robe on and feel all clean, yet kind of vulnerable in a way.

ML: What happens next?

C: We go from there. We travel again. I'm not with the same person now; I have another chaperone. I know this one so well. Now we are in what appears to be a line, like riding an escalator. There are a whole bunch of people, all moving. I see across the way. It appears to be a big circular place with tubes going in carrying people in. There's a huge crowd and they all seem to know where they are going. We go out a different tube. It's weird. It is not the same as having to go to one place after another—places just exist. It feels like you are moving, but you don't know how you got from one place to the other. Now we are going to more familiar territory. It's like when you go to a neighborhood where you grew up. When I recognize where I am, the chaperone leaves me. I thank him.

ML: What do you experience next?
C: I take my time getting where I am going. There's a lot to see. It sounds odd, but it's like a neighborhood. There is a particular house. I don't know if it is yellow or red. It feels like I belong in this house. There is a wooden gate, a cobblestone path, and the door is open. Everyone in the house cheers when I come in. They have been waiting for me. There are hugs and smiles. It is a big family.
ML: Do you recognize anyone there that you have met in this life?
C: Yes, my friend Jake is there. I am glad we are here together again. I am comfortable with most everyone here; it's a group tribe. I have a place to stay. We don't have to eat, but we eat together anyway. It's like we're playing house. I like to experience the closeness of the family. It's funny that there would be a big house in the spirit world.
ML: What we experience as physical in the spiritual world is our projection of the experience. Your experience is real, but the way you perceive it is imagination.
C: I spend a lot of time resting because I just came home. I sleep a lot. Some of my friends come and visit one at a time. A couple of the people in the house are a little more mature. We sit around the table and talk about life. They are not pushy, but they have a strong presence. They know a lot. They tell me I did really well—I did a good job expressing love to the child I raised. I could learn to forgive in my heart more. They ask me a little about where I will choose to go for my next life. That makes me anxious. I want to take a break and not think about what to do next. They are not disapproving, but I'm intimidated by them. I am not feeling very capable. They have a lot of personal power; they are solid on the inside. There is a groundedness I don't have yet. It is nice to have that kind of strength. I'm working on it. They pat me on the shoulder. I know they love me. There are two of them. One is thicker than the other: denser and grounded and strong. The other one is female and she is more mature than I am. They are not parental, just older, like older siblings who watch over me and give me good examples. I think I am known for being childlike, mischievous, and extremely curious. I like to sneak up on people, not to scare them, but as a little game.
ML: What else do you notice about this experience?
C: We talk about whether I want to be a woman or a man next time. It depends. Being a female can sometimes be so much harder. Maybe I'll take a break and have a male body. The experience is so rich in the way that love is experienced and the way you feel in community. It feels richer, fuller, and emotionally broader. My guide opens a book. He is showing me stories, like fairy tales. It's an imaginary place in another dimension. I think he is showing me places I can go. It's like a travel brochure. If I want, I can be in this story, this place. You can do so much in the spirit world, create so many things. It's not the same as the earth experience, but you can learn a lot about yourself through the roles. Not all stories are so much fun. We explore different kinds of scenarios and roles, we see different perspectives, multi-dimensional. It is a good way to develop a sense of empathy.
ML: Move forward through your experiences in the spiritual world, to just before you chose this body. What are your experiences at that time?
C: I am excited about this one. I get to be the youngest child. I have to pay attention to the type of body that I choose. The circuitry will be important. Each body is different. One of the reasons I chose this body is that it has the capability for powerful projection and imagination, extreme sensitivity to the energies around it and of other people. It is able to relax, although there are times when it has difficulty with that. There are more reasons why this body is suitable. Sensitivity is one reason. I can use that to

communicate inner dimensions to people. It makes life harder though, to be so sensitive; one gets distracted and overwhelmed. There were other bodies I could have chosen but none had this sensitivity. If I'm in an intimidating body I can't help people to recognize what's deep down inside them.

Pre-Birth Choices and Experience

The experiences that we have before being born are many and varied. As is true in any phase of existence, many choices must be considered. Our decision-making skills will be called to task; they may be the single most important factor in choosing the time and location of a lifetime.

Choosing our birth time and place can be highly complicated. It involves choosing parents, environment, siblings, opportunities, location, and date. We may consider the prospective parent's health and genetic makeup, or we may be concerned about astrological influences and the numerology of the date or the name.

Strategies of birth can be as complex as a game of chess or as simple as picking a lottery number and crossing our fingers. Ultimately, it is always our personal choice.

Sensing the situation

Most people who have recalled their pre-birth period report having some notion about the parents and the environment into which they have chosen to be born. When people remember their time in the womb, they generally report some degree of clarity about their mother's emotions, and they can interpret the feelings of each parent toward themselves. As an embryo, one typically has memories of conversations, arguments, activities, events, and situations, pleasant or unpleasant. We know whether we feel wanted or loved, and we are aware if there is fear, or anger about the pregnancy, or if an abortion has been desired or attempted.

Can we make mistakes?

It is possible to make an erroneous judgment when choosing a set of parents. Many factors can contribute to this. Sometimes the baby's spirit is simply not paying attention to the details, and she slips into the first available body.

But even with careful consideration, a mistake can be made. Perhaps a couple appeared as though they would provide a good family option. The parents may have been getting along fine without a child; however, with the stress of having a baby, things may begin to fall apart. There might be financial struggles, tension, abuse, divorce, or some other disadvantage.

On the other hand, a spirit may want so desperately to be with a specific person that it is willing to attach itself to a newly forming embryo despite the disadvantages. The mother may be a mere child or she may be unfit in some other way. In this case, the spirit can make a severe mistake by allowing itself to be blinded by emotion.

A client with a difficult family life wanted to understand why she made the choice to be part of that family. She learned that she loved both her parents deeply and wanted them to learn about love. She knew they were not getting along very well, and she had high hopes that when she was born the parents would focus on their love for her and thus overcome their own dysfunctional relationship. Unfortunately, the plan backfired. The birth of the baby brought on much deeper problems between them, and their anger and abuse was taken out on the baby girl. Having this information didn't make the client's life experiences any less damaging for her, but the knowledge allowed her to view her choice as a heroic act of love and purpose.

Our common purpose

The one common purpose that all humans share is to ensure the continuance of our consciousness and our existence. Without consciousness and existence, our souls cannot continue. We enhance our existence and expand our consciousness through varied experiences, both pleasant and challenging. In general, the more challenging the circumstances we face, the greater are the growth opportunities available to us.

This is an exercise I often give to my clients: Each day ask yourself, "How am I feeding my consciousness, my soul, today?" and "How am I ensuring my existence?"

Losing the way

What if we make a choice that sets us on another path? What will happen if that path has nothing to do with our purpose? Moving off course may slow us down, but we can still learn something. Looking at the motivation behind a decision or course of action will help your clients discover an important aspect of their personalities. Doing so also reveals the value system very clearly. Wherever we are in the past or the present, there is always something to learn if we just look around.

The soul has so many lessons to learn. Soon we'll be able to mark off our list whatever lesson we are experiencing right now. If we are learning generosity rather than loyalty, then we can learn loyalty another time. Generosity is a fine thing to have learned. The only real mistake is to *stop* learning or growing. Like our bodies, our souls thrive on constant feeding.

Making Decisions

The decision to return to a physical body is generally made by the soul or spirit. How is that decision made? The way we make decisions in this present life is probably an accurate reflection of the way we make decisions on many other levels of our consciousness. In helping your clients analyze their decision-making strategies, you might ask some questions.

Does your client weigh things out carefully when making decisions, or does he act on impulse? When choosing to come into a body, some souls listen carefully to their counselors, try to evaluate the future consequences of their choices, and determine what lessons might be presented and the overall gain a given lifetime may provide for them. These souls observe the parents, calculate the effect of the siblings and the environment, and extrapolate the opportunities and the challenges available. They use this information to arrive at a rational decision.

Other souls find themselves conflicted about the decision. There are pros and cons involved in coming into any body and, more specifically, into the body in question. These souls may not want to incarnate again, yet they are being advised to do so because the lessons will be valuable or because they have a purpose to fulfill. They may halfheartedly agree to experience this particular lifetime; maybe they feel they are being pushed into the decision. The following transcript, which we first saw in chapter 1, demonstrates a soul agreeing to an incarnation that will be difficult for her.

ML: Now go back to before you were born, to the time when you were deciding to choose this lifetime. What do you remember about that?

C: Someone has a hand, pointing to two people. He is saying something that I can't understand.

ML: There is a part of you that knows fully what it was that he meant. What do you know about what he was communicating to you?

C: He says if you go down there, you can help them. They have tried before and couldn't conceive. They don't want to adopt. Having me as their baby would be good for them and for me.

ML: Why would it be good for you?

C: Because there is someone waiting for me. It isn't them. Someone else. He says, "These people are to have you." There is some difficulty in life that I needed to fix for them. He tells me, "Don't be scared whatever happens. Always be happy. They may not be perfect, but they need someone in their lives." I regretted it at first. I didn't want to leave where I was. But he told me that I had to go. He said they would bring me something that I needed. I had to be with them. There was a plan for me, something waiting for me. When I asked him about that, he said that there had been a mistake and it needed to be fixed. When I asked what that had to do with me, he told me they are a part of me. He wants to help these other people so I said I would do it. He says that there is something wrong, but that I am doing good. The darkness that was going to come hasn't yet.

Some souls move through the process blindly, not thinking clearly about, or even paying attention to, the details of their options. They are seeking the fulfillment of other needs. Perhaps they have unresolved addictions—drugs, alcohol, sex, relationships, food, shopping, physical body sensations, and so forth—and they now simply crave any opportunity to return to old habits. Still other souls may not be comfortable out of a physical body. They may be afraid of what they are experiencing and eager to return to something more familiar. Later on in this chapter, I give a description of my father's sojourn between bodies, and you will notice some of these issues as he goes through the process of moving forward on his soul's journey.

You may want to assist your clients in examining their decision-making skills. Their ability to use a balanced process in approaching choices may give them an advantage when choosing their next lifetime. Ask your client to consider how the decisions she made when coming into this present body are reflected in her situation, in her parents, in her opportunities, and in the challenges she has faced. The answers to these questions can give important clues regarding the lessons she may face and the purpose she is attempting to fulfill.

Do people choose violent families?

Sometimes a person thinks he is choosing a good situation and then it goes sour. It might simply be a mistake, but in some cases the spirit has chosen to come into a lifetime that he knows will involve violence. This decision can be based on the need to fulfill a purpose, not a simple desire to experience violence. The soul may be trying, perhaps unsuccessfully, to teach the power of love over violence. Or the soul may choose to put himself into a difficult situation to teach his parent the consequences of violence, consequences which may include incarceration, regret, and other karmic repercussions. In other cases, the child may choose a difficult situation to teach himself the effects of pain and provide himself the opportunity to learn compassion, strength, independence, nonviolence, or fairness.

Occasionally a dysfunctional spirit will incarnate, coming into a difficult situation with the express purpose of reinforcing negative behaviors, and thus giving itself justification for future violent behavior. Although this may seem extraordinary to the average person, sadly, it is true. Dysfunctional spirits may include souls who incarnated and became serial killers or warmongers. For example, imagine what the future lifetimes of Charles Manson, Adolph Hitler, Osama bin Laden, or Saddam Hussein would be like, if they were not truly rehabilitated before death.

There aren't many case studies to substantiate the concept of dysfunctional spirits because most people who are interested in past life regression are also interested in spiritual growth. Those souls who choose to justify their violence would have a hard time facing the information they would discover during a hypnosis session. If a person like this does agree to go through such therapy, he is likely well on his way to making positive changes in his consciousnesses.

Choosing lessons, not families

Sometimes a spirit is not as concerned about her birth family; instead her focus is on having specific opportunities or lessons for the growth of her soul. In this case, the goal is to accomplish a purpose rather than to be with specific people.

An individual may have many different levels of purpose and a multitude of reasons for her choices. When a soul makes the decision to come into a certain life based on a desire to accomplish a specific life goal, she is choosing a situation, possibly a challenging one, that will promote her spiritual growth. Such a decision can grant a person an existence that is ultimately more enjoyable and valuable, and can promote the expansion of her consciousness. It is true that when we live with our shortcomings and failures we live in a sort of hell, whereas when we courageously face the difficult challenges in our lives, we create heaven.

While it is possible for a spirit to learn while in the astral, the testing of new knowledge happens specifically during a physical manifestation. The superconscious mind of the spirit is fully cognizant of all the lessons the individual soul requires, but it can be difficult for the soul to do that self-reflection on its own. When deciding on the next life, therefore, spirit guides are often brought into the discussion to help with the decision-making process.

It can be a daunting decision to enter into a difficult or challenging lifetime. Yet avoiding your lessons only prolongs the process and may draw other challenges to you. All the lessons eventually have to be learned by every individual. There can be ways to learn faster or easier, but nonetheless, the tests truly have to be passed. There is no faking it. If we claim to have learned a certain lesson, but we are really only avoiding facing up to it, the lesson will simply reappear in another lifetime. The subconscious mind will continue to provide opportunities for us to get it right.

Once we have passed a test, it will no longer be noticed. We will cruise through a similar situation without even noticing a bump in the road. Until then, even if we die in the learning process, the same obstacle will continue to present an opportunity to learn.

A Personal Experience

While writing this book, I was gifted with the opportunity to observe my father's transition from being a vital, active man, through death, and into his reentrance into this world as a healthy baby girl.

Within a year of being diagnosed with mesothelioma, a deadly cancer related to asbestos exposure, my father was dying in a hospice center. Before he died, my brother and I had the opportunity to talk everything over thoroughly with Dad, making sure, repeatedly, that we had resolved everything possible between us. Although he was not certain that he believed in reincarnation, he was curious about anything that might help him during the final phase of his life. Since reincarnation, past lives, and journeying between lives is my area of interest and experience, I gave him every piece of valuable information I could. I also told him that it didn't matter whether he believed what I was telling him, I was simply offering information to file away in case it served him at some point, in this life or after. We spoke about this for a while, and he told me that he hoped I was right. He still was not entirely convinced, and that was all right. I was happy to know that he had the information in case it ever came in handy. Having this discussion comforted me personally, since I knew I had shared everything I knew that might help my father make his transition.

Three weeks after being placed in the hospice facility, my father died quietly and comfortably. The rest of the story I learned from psychic intuition, meditation, and information given to me by my spirit guides. My guides and my father's guides were there when he died, taking his hand and comforting him as he made the transition. He appeared a bit surprised to discover that there really was more to life than his physical existence. He was somewhat disoriented, so he was surrounded by friendly spirit guides who watched over him, conversed with him, instructed him, and protected him.

For some unknown reason, my father had amnesia concerning his most recent lifetime. When I visited him in the astral, he did not recognize me as his daughter Mary Lee, but rather as his daughter Annabelle from the 1700s or as his teacher from a more ancient lifetime. For two months he stayed in that condition, not recognizing his family or remembering the experiences from his most recent lifetime.

My spirit guides shifted his experience of time and were able to give him instruction and healing for the equivalent of three Earth years, even though only one night passed on Earth. Afterward, he regained full consciousness of this lifetime and was able to visit us. Whenever he visited me, I felt a low-level electrical vibration moving through my right hand. It was very distinct and could draw my attention away from other things I was doing. Even with the instruction he was receiving and his companionship with me, my father was not content to remain in the astral plane. He wanted to return to a physical body as soon as possible.

On a Wednesday morning in mid-February, three months after his death, I woke up sad, teary-eyed, heartbroken, and missing my dad. My spirit guides informed me that Dad had decided to incarnate into a baby the following weekend, so I would have a couple of days to say my goodbyes for this lifetime.

In meditation, I discovered that he was born as a baby girl the following Sunday morning. Within a day or two, however, he began to regret his selection of bodies. He could envision the path that would be available to him and also the limitations that this course presented, and he did not like this choice at all. The baby contracted severe complications and died. Immediately he chose another baby girl's body and was born again, three to four days later. She is doing well on her new path, and her astrology chart is very spiritual and adventuresome. She appears to be very satisfied with her present course.

It is glorious to think of my dad now, in a fresh new body, enjoying the love of new parents and the prospects of upcoming adventures in the physical world. Furthermore, this story illuminates some facts about the death and rebirth process that may help you support your clients as they deal with issues of preparing for their own deaths, or the deaths of loved ones. The story of my father contains some crucial points. Consider the following:

An individual's spirit does not have to attach to the fetus at conception.

My father did not make a final, permanent attachment until two days prior to his birth (This detail has interesting implications regarding public opinion of abortions).

He was only between lives for three months before choosing to reincarnate.

He did not become omniscient upon death; in fact, he experienced amnesia.

After death, he was consciously present around me for only a short period. He didn't instantly become my spirit guide or a permanent advisor from the other side.

My father will not necessarily be present and waiting for my mother when she returns to the astral. Although some people may choose to wait for their spouses, this is not always the case.

My father is now focused on his new life, as we are focused on our own present lives. He is no longer concerned about former loved ones who remain here. None of us spend a lot of time and effort thinking about family from our most recent past life. We move on.

Even after being reborn, my father still had the opportunity to change his mind. This detail may offer additional understanding concerning infant deaths.

My dad had led an honorable life, free of addictions or abuse. His choice to reincarnate was based more on personal comfort than on compulsion. Although Dad did not enjoy his time in the astral plane, most people enjoy it very much. A significant number of people report being hesitant to return to a physical body because they prefer their experiences in the astral.

The process of tracking of a spirit's movement, as I did with my father, gives me some new ideas about the story of Jesus and the three wise men. Perhaps the three wise men did not simply follow a star in the sky. In some stories, they are portrayed as magicians (Magi) rather than kings, and they might have been of the druidic lineage, able to read the astrological stars. Maybe they were capable, as well, of psychic vision, astral projection, communicating with their spirit guides, and many other forms of phenomenal sensing. Truly, we are all capable of using these powers. Could they have known the spirit of Jesus from the astral or from previous incarnations? And were they already aware of his plans to incarnate? It would be easy for the Magi to ascertain that Jesus was choosing to incarnate in a general location on a certain date. The wise men's psychic sensing could have drawn them close to the location of the birth, where they would simply inquire about recent births and then look at the astrological chart of the child to know his identity. Of course when they found the child and were in his presence, it would have been obvious to men with such awareness that this particular child held the spirit they were seeking. Such questions and musings will surely come to you as you work with your clients. Past life regression work keeps us inquiring as to the nature of the universe, and as to our own nature, and that is as it should be.

CHAPTER EIGHT
Techniques for Healing During Regression

During a regression session, many issues may arise that continue to affect the client adversely to the present day. These issues may appear in the client's present life in many ways: an unexplained pain, a block to achieving desired goals, undesirable behaviors and emotional responses, or disease. A number of techniques can be used in the midst of a past life regression that will greatly benefit the client, offering healing and change that can liberate the person from the results of past life events.

These techniques can include Object Imagery, Secondary Gains, Parts Therapy, Chair Therapy, Reframing, Desensitization, and others. All are addressed fully in my book *Hypnotherapy: A Client-Centered Approach*. I will not repeat that material here. Instead, I will give examples of how some of these techniques can be used within a session by offering examples of case studies.

Removing Blocks

A client has been working steadily on her life journey and has recognized some inner subconscious blocks that are causing her trouble. Her goal in reviewing her past lives is to gain an understanding about her own nature and character, and to remove any barriers that would prevent her from moving forward in attaining her life goals.

ML: What do you notice about the door?

C: It is a rich, textured wood, with squares, and each square has a knob in the center. The door is natural, unvarnished wood that has been hand rubbed. There is an ornate brass handle, and the molding is carved with oak leaves, acorns, and flowers. It's rich, heavy and gleaming. There are candles flickering in the hall. The walls are satiny and smooth.

ML: As the door opens and you move through the threshold, what do you notice?

C: I'm indoors. There is a man sitting at a small wooden table that looks like a desk. On a card table is a glass candlestick with a finger loop. It holds a beeswax candle. The man is writing in ink on a parchment sheet whose edges are held down with rocks. There is an inkwell, a quill and some more goose feathers, a knife, and a pewter cup.

ML: What else do you notice?

C: We are in a bedchamber with a four-poster bed. There are curtains, which are pulled tight at night, and an Indian rug. The walls are covered in red silk and wainscoting. This man is intense at his work. He is older, with gray-white hair and a Vandyke beard. He is my father.

ML: What do you know about yourself?

C: I'm female, about nine years old.

ML: As I count down from three to one, you will know where in the world you are. Three, two, one . . . where are you?

C: We are in London.

ML: As I count from three to one, you will know what the date is. Three, two, one . . . what is the date?

C: 1420.

ML: What else do you notice about this scene?

C: I wish my father would pay more attention to me, but he is doing something very important. It seems to be political. Finally he reaches a hand out to me and I walk to him. He puts his arm around me, holding me, but he is still writing. Now I feel better because he knows that I am here. He looks like William Shakespeare.

ML: Do you recognize him as anyone you know in this lifetime?

C: Maybe he is my father in this life. It feels like the same connection. It's deep, there is a thread between us.

ML: What do you notice about that thread?

C: It's gold, with colors. It appears to be a mere filament, thin, ephemeral. It stretches to my dad in this life, too, even though he is now deceased.

ML: What else do you notice?

C: Now we are outside, and my father is giving a speech from a wooden platform. People don't agree with him, and they say awful things. I'm on some wooden stairs or a ladder of sorts. I'm 16 now, and I understand how important his message is. He's telling people about tyranny and the yoke of oppression, and I think that I should be doing that, too. The people have only to change their minds and be free, but they don't want to believe it is that simple. There are spies in the audience. I fear that my father will get hurt, and I think that if only I weren't a female, I could help him. I'm frustrated to be a female. Maybe I could help him even so, but it won't be easy. It's not the right time for his message. They will hang him for sedition if he doesn't get away. What a relief! He gets away! It's night. I see torches and feel the heat on my face. But I know my father got away and I'll be taken care of. I should be scared but I'm not. It's as though I'm invisible to them, they can't see me. Since I'm a female, it doesn't occur to them that I could be a problem. My mind is working, though.

ML: What do you notice next?

C: Now I'm in America. I'm frustrated again, really angry. It's a different life, this is 1764 and I'm 15 years old. I'm with my father, who is wearing a blue suit with a white shirt and collar. He's a lawyer, and he tells me I can do anything I want, he believes in me. Then my mother comes in and tells him not to put such thoughts into my head. My mother is a vacuous woman in a fancy dress. She thinks I should learn to be a good wife. My father acquiesces so I have to go to the dance, where I'm expected to flutter my eyelashes and act stupid. I don't like this at all. I must figure out whom to listen to, whom to trust. No wonder I feel so strongly now, no wonder I can't sell myself short. It matters to me what happens. I'm tired of wasting time and energy.

ML: What else do you notice?

C: I end up getting married to a cruel man who does ugly things in bed. I bear his children. I pine for myself and then die of a broken heart.

ML: Moving to another life that will give us additional information, where do you find yourself next?

C: I'm in a big, comfortable room, and I'm happy. The large windows are open and there are French doors, like windows. I'm female. I'm at a desk, writing. I've put purposelessness away. I do what I need to do for myself and for my own knowledge. I have a sense that these stories I write will be universal. They're about humanity—essential humanity—about connecting, kindness, and inclusion. I've left politics behind; my writing is not hard-edged stuff, instead it connects to the feminine and the gentle side of life.

ML: What else do you notice?

C: My gown is soft and easy to wear, empire style, something like Josephine might have worn. I'm in France and it is 1894. I'm in a cottage outside Paris in the Bois du Boulogne. There are pine trees. It's nice being a woman. (She laughs.) I am married to an army captain with whom I feel safe. I can write when I want to write. Oh, he's my next-door neighbor in this lifetime, and now he's a United States Air Force Captain. Interesting!

ML: What else do you notice?

C: This life is so much easier and much less painful. I write from happiness. Could that happen? (Chuckles) We're just happy. What a novel idea! I finish writing and put down the pen. Now I feel I've done something good.

ML: What have you learned from reviewing this lifetime?

C: I want no more fighting. There will be no more raging against the gods; it's too hard and leads to disaster. I'm a woman and I have to embrace the feminine. It is okay for me to relax and feel protected. I want to get a fuller understanding of what I've been seeing, My speech is hopeful, attractive, and magnetic. I can put a positive spin on things. It seems as though I am offering the carrot, but it's deeper. When there is a problem, I can intuit what to do so the outcome is positive for everyone involved. I understand myself to be like a gardener: I make a decision and then perpetuate it.

This client's perceptions, imagination, and memories are articulated in wonderful detail. She is an easy subject and moves smoothly from lifetime to lifetime. Not all clients have this ability. From this session, she has gained information that will help her with her life work, her personality, her courage, and her sensuality.

Object Imagery and Reverse Metaphor

Object Imagery can be used as a simple way to initiate a past life regression. Additionally, in the midst of a regression it can be used to alter or eliminate a pain that resulted from a past life experience.

To use Object Imagery, when a client comes to the office complaining of a physical pain or sensation, for example, simply ask him to close his eyes, take a breath, relax, and focus on the sensation. Ask him to describe the sensation in detail. Then ask him to create a metaphorical object that represents the sensation, or one that could cause the sensation.

The following is a sample of typical language that you may use when utilizing this technique. Of course you will substitute body parts or descriptions that fit the individual client.

Close your eyes. Take a deep breath, and as you exhale, allow yourself to relax as deeply as you can. Take another breath, exhale, and begin to focus on that pain in your shoulder. Please describe the pain so that if I had that pain, I would know it was just like yours.

If the client is not very articulate, you may ask him whether the pain is sharp or dull, constant or throbbing, deep or on the surface, burning or cold, and so on.

If the pain had a shape and a color, if it were an object, what would it look like? If an object was creating this sensation, what would it look like?

If he still seems to be struggling to find an answer, you may ask: "Imagine that I have handed you a picture of yourself and some crayons. I would like you to draw the pain on the picture so that by looking at it, I would know what you are experiencing. How would you draw that?"

Once the image has been established, ask the client to tell you a story about how it got there. This initiates a technique termed Reverse Metaphor. The following transcript demonstrates these techniques.

A female client came to the office with a long list of issues. She had had a tumor in her ear several years ago, and she claimed the operation took her smile away. Along with headaches and dizziness, she sensed a blockage in her first and second chakras (the energy centers relating to the tailbone and genital areas). "I'm holding on to something," she stated. Two weeks before our session she had experienced her colon spasms worsening, and she declared, "Nothing moves through me." She has a history of eating disorders, and she described an internal trauma with food.

Because she was experiencing a headache at the time of our session, we began the session with Object Imagery. Although the visualization began as a metaphor, it quickly became apparent that it was a past life regression.

ML: Focus on the pain of your headache. If those sensations had a shape and color, what would they look like?
C: It looks like a green bubble, like a solid ball with a rope tied tightly around the middle. It's pulling to the left.
ML: If you could communicate with it telepathically, what would it tell you about why it is

there?
- C: It has something to do with the physical and something to do with the emotions.
- ML: What would you like to do with it?
- C: I want to relax it, but I can't seem to do that.
- ML: I would like to ask the subconscious mind to provide your conscious mind with a metaphor, a story, that will give us information and insight into the origins and purpose of this green bubble. As I count from three to one, you may begin telling me the story. Three, two, one. Does your story begin indoors or outdoors?
- C: Indoors.
- ML: What else do you notice about your surroundings?
- C: It is nighttime. It's a dark place, confining, a cold, damp dungeon.
- ML: If you were in the story, would you be a man or a woman?
- C: I'm a man.
- ML: And how old do you feel?
- C: Twenty-five.
- ML: What else do you know about your situation?
- C: I'm being punished for stealing. I had very abusive parents, so I ran away and had to steal to survive. There was no work for me. My little sister was with me, too.
- ML: When you look at your little sister and feel her energy, do you recognize her as anyone you know in this lifetime?
- C: She is my husband in this lifetime. I'm protecting her. We are so hungry! I have hurt someone, I stabbed him in the side of the head. I didn't kill him, but I left him with a scar on the side of the face. Now I am in prison and my sister has to fend for herself. I feel so much guilt, but there is nothing I can do about it; I have to suffer the consequences. My sister has forgiven me, she understands and manages to get through it. Because I took care of her in that lifetime, she has now come back as my husband to take care of me. I die peacefully in jail in that life. I don't live long at all.
- ML: Imagine the man that you stabbed standing in front of you there. What do you notice about him?
- C: He is young and blonde, rich and spoiled. He is very angry with me. He owns a bakery and he doesn't want to share anything. I wasn't asking for food, just for scraps, but he won't give me anything at all. It angers me so because we are both the same age, yet I'm deprived of his lifestyle. I go crazy and slash at his face; he buckles up and curses me. I run and hide, but they find me. I have taken away some of his perfect life, and now he won't forgive me.
- ML: Look even deeper at him. What does he really want?
- C: In his soul, he wants to be forgiven by me. He asks me to forgive him for not giving us any food. I forgive him and tell him that I am sorry. He forgives me, begrudgingly. I find it difficult to accept apologies.
- ML: What did this episode allow him to learn in that lifetime?
- C: He learned that he shouldn't judge people by their appearances. He should have extended himself and not been so self-centered. He needed to understand that we are all brothers, and he says he's learning this lesson in another lifetime. He tells me that my actions moved him along faster because after the disfiguring, people looked at him differently. They had to look beyond his beauty. Because of this, he has become a more caring person, he is learning. He is not as attractive in this lifetime, and that is okay. Now he is forgiving me and I am becoming more relaxed; my body is more relaxed.
- ML: Picture the 25-year-old that was you in that lifetime. What do you know about him

now?

C: The stabbing was not good, but what he did for his sister was good. He protected her and provided for her unselfishly. Although he was being so selfless, he became frustrated. His intention was good but he needed to let go of anger at another person, which he had been storing and carrying around. He was unhappy at that time and felt that life was unjust, but he was creating more tension and, therefore, creating certain circumstances. He knows it's true. He had to learn his lessons, so he chose that experience.

ML: Did he learn what he needed to?

C: He learned a lot of lessons, but not the one about letting go of resentment and anger. He also needs to forgive his parents from that lifetime, and he needs to thank them.

ML: Why would he thank them?

C: Because the circumstances of his life allowed him to learn independence and love. When he lashed out, he severed his spiritual contact. He had to learn that life is not a punishment. I want to forgive him.

ML: Can you do that?

C: I have forgiven him now. It makes me feel light.

ML: What are you noticing now?

CL: I see a rainbow and clouds. I'm a being of light whose work on Earth is to bring joy. Life is colorful. My spirit guides and angels are always there, streaking across the sky and making halos. I, too, can streak across the sky and be delightfully colorful. I can keep my eyes wide open. I don't have to be so harsh on myself and others, I can be in the moment, in joy and peace.

ML: Is there anything else?

C: I will be able to recognize when others have pain. Because I have been there myself, I can help others recognize their pain. I don't have to change myself or anyone else, I can accept them and love them, starting with myself. I have such gratitude for this day, it has been an epiphany for me. Anytime I sense tension, I can just breathe in the rainbow.

This client experienced relief from her physical symptoms right away, and she received a visual anchor that will allow her to create similar states of mind in the future.

Secondary Gains, Parts Therapy, and Outcomes

There are many techniques that promote health and well-being for our clients. My purpose in this section is not to describe the techniques in detail, but to allow you to see them in action through a transcript.

A client came in with weight issues, a desire to know about her life's purpose, and the wish to bolster her self-esteem. Due to various stresses, she had gained about 40 pounds over the past few months. Although she has been extremely successful in her career, she now wants to leave her job and begin her own business. All these issues are tied together and lead into exploring past lives, so I am presenting the entire transcript. We start by addressing the presenting problem, the weight issue.

ML: Taking a breath and closing your eyes, begin to imagine that you are in a pool of still water. Any ripples you may notice in the pool are in response to your thought patterns and energy. As you continue to observe the pool, relaxing deeper and deeper, you will notice that the ripples become calmer and less frequent. As a part of your mind continues to observe the pool, relaxing, I would like to ask another part of your mind to answer four questions (Secondary Gains). Remain relaxed yet able to speak, and please tell me what carrying the extra weight allows you to do.

C: It allows me to hide. I don't have to do things that are risky.

ML: What does carrying the extra weight prevent you from doing?

C: It prevents me from doing risky things, even those things that I am capable of and that are good for me.

ML: If you did not carry the extra weight around, what would that allow you to do?

C: I'd feel more confident about being in the public eye. I would stand up and be heard. I would move out of my comfort zone.

ML: What would not carrying the extra weight prevent you from doing?

C: I can't think of anything.

ML: Is it true that there is a part of you that wants to lose the extra weight and another part of you that, for whatever reason, resists losing it? (Introducing Part Therapy)

C: Definitely.

ML: Imagine separating those two parts distinctly, so that the part of you that wants to lose weight is on one hand and the part that resists losing weight is on the other hand. Which hand wants to lose the weight?

C: The right hand.

ML: And the left had resists it?

C: Yes.

ML: Allow your focus to move into the right hand, the hand that wants to lose the weight. If it had a soap box to stand on so that it could tell me whatever it wanted in order to convince me of its position, what would it tell me?

C: It could tell you a bunch of things: I could be an active participant and a leader in various issues. I would have a voice and be listened to. People would feel different after hearing me. I could make a big difference. I would coach people about their potential, give them positive self-belief. I would have a great life and reach my own potential. This is good—and fun! I feel fabulous, I can do anything at all!

ML: Come out of the right hand and over to the left hand. What would it have to say?

C: Why would you want to do that? It could be embarrassing. Who would listen to you? What makes you think you have anything to say? What makes you so special? Don't draw attention to yourself. It's better to take the tried and true path, the clear and dependable path that you can count on. There's no need to rock the boat. Life is already really good now.

ML: How would the right hand respond to that?

C: Life is short. Let's have some fun, let's stir things up a bit! The only way to get your confidence up is to do it.

ML: How does the left hand respond to that?

C: Life will become very different. Are you sure you want to take that risk? Look at all you might lose.

ML: How does the right hand respond?

C: It banged the left over the head! It says look how much I have to gain. I have never been frightened before.

ML: How does the left hand respond?

C: It's your call.

ML: And the right?

C: It's quiet. Yep. Life's too short for regret.

ML: And the left's response?

C: It shrugged. Okay, it's your call.

ML: How does the right respond?

C: Watch me fly!

ML: Does the left hand want to support the right, or does it just get out of the way?

C: It wants to hang around and check that I don't hurt myself. It doesn't want me to fly too far too fast. It wants to watch from the sidelines.

ML: What is the goal of the left hand in holding back and watching? (Introducing Outcomes)

C: (Burst of tears and emotion.) It wants me to succeed!

ML: If you could succeed, fully and completely as you imagine it now, then what would you have that is even more important?

C: I'd be doing good things and making a difference for a lot of people.

ML: If you could make a difference for a lot of people, fully and completely as you imagine it now, then what would you have that is even more important?

C: I'd be really proud.

ML: If you could be really proud, fully and completely as you imagine it now, then what would you have that is even more important?

C: I would have the freedom to do what I want, when and where I want it.

ML: If you had the freedom to do what you want, fully and completely as you imagine it now, then what would you have that is even more important?

C: I'd have time to spend with people I love, room for more people, time for my garden, time for playing and being with children.

ML: If you had time to spend with others, fully and completely as you imagine it now, then what would you have that is even more important?

C: I'd have a sense of peace and contentment. It's warm, cozy, and calm.

ML: As you experience that sensation of peace and contentment, allow it to intensify. I would like to ask the subconscious mind to produce a symbol for you that represents this feeling. What is that symbol? (Empowerment Symbol)
C: A star.
ML: If you were to carry that star and this feeling of peace and contentment with you into each and every moment of the future, how would that change your experience of having time to spend with others? (Continuing with Outcomes)
C: It would remind me of what is important. I would be very clear that I want more of that kind of time.
ML: If you were to carry that star and this feeling of peace and contentment with you into each and every moment of the future, how would that change your experience of the freedom to do what you want?
C: I would have a wee secret that I could cuddle close, one that would remind me and restore me. It would let me know that what I am doing is absolutely the best thing, that it is right.
ML: If you were to carry that star and this feeling of peace and contentment with you into each and every moment of the future, how would that change your experience of being proud?
C: I would be able to be openly proud rather than privately. I wouldn't brush off compliments.
ML: If you were to carry that star and this feeling of peace and contentment with you into each and every moment of the future, how would that change your experience of doing good things?
C: I would be more comfortable and confident when sticking my neck out and getting involved. It would polish the star.
ML: If you were to carry that star and this feeling of peace and contentment with you into each and every moment of the future, how would that change your experience of succeeding?
C: I would take more risks.
ML: If you were to carry that star and this feeling of peace and contentment with you into each and every moment of the future, how would that change your experience of carrying the extra weight?
C: I can get rid of it. It slows me down and holds me back.
ML: What does the left hand have to say now? (Continuing with Parts Therapy)
C: It's sad. It wants to hang around.
ML: What can you do about that?
C: It can be in the audience cheering. It would say, "I knew her when. Didn't she do well?" It would have a front row seat.
ML: How is the right hand feeling now?
C: Responsible. It has to be vigilant and really deliver. It feels liberated as well.
ML: Is there any part of you that would resist losing the weight now?
C: No.
ML: Imagine drawing the energy of the right side over to the left side, balancing the energies across your body. How does that feel?
C: Tired, calm, and yet bubbly and fizzy.

ML: I would like to ask the subconscious mind now to provide past life experiences that will help you understand your life purpose more fully. Imagine a hallway stretching out before you. As you move down along the hall, you begin to notice the texture of the floor covering beneath your feet and the color of the walls. There are doorways along this hall, each one leading to past lives, memories, that will help you understand your life purpose. As I count from three to one, you will find yourself in front of one of these doors. Three, two, one. How would you describe the door you are standing in front of now?

C: It is a white cottage door with glass squares and a brass knob.

ML: As the door opens and you move through, where do you find yourself?

C: It's bright. I feel uplifted.

ML: As your eyes become adjusted to the brightness, you begin to discern shapes and colors. What do you begin to notice?

C: Oh! I think I am in heaven. I see bright light, so pure and enveloping. It's drawing me in. I see someone above me. Is it God? He's sending down light; I see his face above me in the light, and I'm not frightened. God makes me into an angel, puts light around me, and turns me around. Now he is sending me back. He is smiling and encouraging, and he waves as I go. I feel sad about leaving, walking away from the light. I see myself looking back over my shoulder at God's face. He is urging me on with the light, saying, "Okay, it's okay. This will be good." I get to the door and open it, and I'm back in the hall, going down to another door.

ML: What do you notice about this one?

C: It's green, wooden, and paneled. I don't feel good about it. I look back over my shoulder and see the white glass door with the light. I know that I have to go through this other door. So I do.

ML: What do you notice?

C: It's dark and feels cold. There are people with palm fronds urging me forward. I walk into golden sunshine and amazing golden light. I think I'm a queen or something. My hair is black with bangs like Cleopatra. The people are all bowing and falling down. As I turn, I notice that I have a train of material behind me, which swishes to the side. I sit and smile at all the people who are bent down before me. The palm fronds are still waving. It must be warm. I say, "Arise," and the people sit up. All the people are smiling, happy and content because we are a prosperous nation. People come out of the crowd to ask me things. I lean forward and answer them, and they smile and go away. I am wise, very wise. After awhile I get up and walk down the carpet, and all the happy people bow again. I come up to big wooden double doors that form an arch. That disappears and I'm feeling better.

ML: Then what happens?

C: The doors get opened for me. When I go in, I'm wearing a suit with a straight tweed skirt, black shoes with heels, and a boxy jacket. I look like Margaret Thatcher, no more black hair anymore. I go into a business meeting and sit at the head of an oval table covered with papers. There are old, pompous men in dark gray suits at the meeting. I'm making the decisions and they don't think I should be there. I'm quite abrupt with them. Some of the men shift uncomfortably in their seats. "If you don't like it, feel free to leave," I say firmly. A few men smile and nod encouragingly. Then they file out with their papers. I sit on a chair for awhile, drawing deep breaths. I tell myself, "Well, you did that." Someone comes in and I have to go. I sigh and pick up my briefcase, which doesn't match my suit or shoes. That bothers me. I go back to the door that I came in, which is behind the head of the table.

ML: What happens next?

C: As I go through the door, I see bamboo and tortoise shell everywhere. It is very quiet. I see water and butterflies. I'm in a garden, like at a Japanese teahouse, open on one side. I'm standing under the cover of the bamboo trees, looking at some rough stepping-stones. I am wearing a kimono and funny little white socks with sandals, and I am deciding whether I want to walk on the stepping-stones. Farther down there is a bridge. It would be nice to sit on the other side and look at the water. I look around to see if anyone is watching, then I pick up my skirts and fly over the stones and bridge. I sit and listen in case anyone calls for me. It is so peaceful. I'm grabbing a few minutes of solitude before I have to go back and do something. The water flows quietly over the stones and moss. I feel sad because my time is not my own, people are counting on me to go back and do something. I am public property. It's unusual for a woman to be listened to, so I have to be wise with my words. It is a heavy burden, being wise. The people—the men—wait for me to do the wrong thing. But I'm very good friends with the emperor, and because of this people watch me closely. They think I haven't earned my right to be listened to, but I know that what I am doing is important in its own right.

ML: Then what do you notice?

C: I bow at the people and they bow at me. I go off to the doorway but there is no door, just a wooden frame.

ML: As you move through it, where do you find yourself?

C: I'm in a concert hall. It is softly dark and full of people. The men are in tuxedos. I am sitting in the front row near the maestro. I'm tall and elegant, wearing jewels and a green velvet dress with a skirt like a meringue. My long hair is swept up and my eyes glisten. The music is beautiful and I am so happy. I am swept away, transported, moved. My man is very good looking. He gets our coats and puts on his top hat and coat. We sweep down wide stone stairs to a horse and carriage. My skirt is too puffy, and we laugh and laugh, trying to get it into the carriage. He tells me, "It came out of the carriage so it must go back into the carriage." Our driver takes us to a beautiful restaurant with candles and a big dance floor. I believe we are in England. We sweep in. It's all shiny, glittery, with white tablecloths. Just lovely. I'm wearing long gloves past my elbows. I know people here, so I tip my head to them and smile sweetly. We are a golden couple, so happy, and people like to talk about us. Our table is near the dance floor.

ML: What else is going on?

C: I wonder why the people know us. They are friendly yet aloof, very British. We dance and we are so happy. I feel like a princess.

ML: What year is it?

C: 1868.

ML: What is your name?

C: Princess Leonora.

ML: What is your man's name?

C: Michael. We are visiting England from Sweden. We are the guests of honor at a reception. Oh, that's why we were in the front row at the concert, it was put on for us. My family is royalty but Michael's is not. He has a good heart, he's very kind, and he does good things.. We have lots of fun at home, behind the gate, so to speak. We laugh, not like the rest of the family, who are starchy. I have to make a lot of decisions. Now I see myself in a room behind a desk with a big seal and wax. I am not so happy.

ML: Why are you not happy?

C: Michael is not there. He left me. It was too complicated, and he needed more for himself. He went riding, wearing a red sash over one shoulder, and he never came back. For a while people thought he was dead. He did die eventually in a horse riding accident, but not straight away. I never saw him again. My last memory of him was when he was getting on the horse with his red sash. Then I had to be very strong and I didn't laugh so much, but I still had that green dress. Sometimes I would go and snuggle into it. I would hold it and cry.

ML: What have you learned from these lifetimes?

C: I am wise. I have the ability to be very, very happy and to make others happy. I am strong and can be tough when I need to be. I need to have time for myself, too, to play. The need for wisdom and decision-making can weigh heavily on me, but I am absolutely meant to do something with this wisdom. I have lots of it, and God wants me to use it. I'm alone a lot, I feel alone. My decisions affect a lot of people.

ML: How will these lifetimes affect your present life?

C: It gives me confidence and courage so that my present path can be comfortable for me. It is okay to do what I am doing, in fact I almost have to do it. I need to be mindful of keeping something for myself, to save quiet time for friends, and to keep my balance.

We completed the session with one more technique to reinforce her new perceptions of herself. When I spoke with this client some days later, she told me that she was surprised when she was tempted to eat some doughnuts and she easily passed them up. She heard a strong voice within her saying that eating them was not a part of her new path. Seeing the sweets was only a test, she told me, not a temptation to eat.

It is somewhat unusual to have a client go from door to door during a visualization, finding a new lifetime behind each one. This client's session flowed easily; not all sessions are so fluid.

Removing the Analytical Imp

The next case demonstrates a technique that is useful when a client is overly analytical. The client's hyper-alert mind was interfering with her ability to experience the regression. As I guided her through an Outcome Therapy technique, she allowed herself to relax and move into the regression effortlessly. This and other techniques are discussed fully in my book, which is cited at the beginning of this chapter. This technique was first developed and introduced in a book entitled *Core Transformations* by Connirae Andreas with Tamara Andreas. I led this client through a short induction, and then into the hallway visualization.

ML: Describe the door you are standing in front of.
C: It is a Ritz Carlton style hallway, long and nice, with a red carpet.
ML: What does the door look like?
C: I'm not finding a door. When I look for a door, it kind of fades.
ML: Would you say it is true that a part of you wants to relax and experience a regression, and another part of you is analytical and prevents you from relaxing?
C: Yes, that's very true.
ML: I would like to ask the analytical part what its goal is for you.
C: To be right.
ML: If you were right, fully and completely as you imagine it, then what would you have that is even more important?
C: I could finish things.
ML: If you could finish things, fully and completely as you imagine it, then what would you have that is even more important?
C: Accomplishment.
ML: If you had accomplishment, fully and completely as you imagine it, then what would you have that is even more important?
C: I could offer help to the world.
ML: If you could offer help to the world, fully and completely as you imagine it, then what would you have that is even more important?
C: I could do anything.
ML: If you could do anything, fully and completely as you imagine it, then what would you have that is even more important?
C: No rushing. I could be relaxed and stress free. No one would be waiting for me.
ML: If you could be relaxed and stress free, fully and completely as you imagine it, then what would you have that is even more important?
C: My body would feel lighter. It would be like floating.
ML: I would like to ask your subconscious mind to produce a symbol that you can imagine holding in your hand, which represents this good feeling. What is that symbol?
C: A lotus with a star in a bright circle of light.
ML: If you were to carry this lotus star and this light, floating feeling with you into each and every moment of the future, how do you think that might change your experience of not rushing?
C: It wouldn't fit me. It would be too irresponsible.
ML: If you were to carry this lotus star and this light, floating feeling with you into each and every moment of the future, how do you think that might change your experience of being able to do anything?
C: I just could.
ML: If you were to carry this lotus star and this light, floating feeling with you into each and every moment of the future, how do you think that might change your experience of giving help to the world?
C: I would be able to influence my corner of the world.
ML: If you were to carry this lotus star and this light, floating feeling with you into each and every moment of the future, how do you think that might change your experience of accomplishment?
C: I would follow through on my projects and my work.

ML: With the goal of following through with your desire to experience a past life regression, would your analytical part be willing to allow you to relax and enjoy this adventure, so that it will later have even more information to analyze?
C: Sure.
ML: Going back into that hallway, how would you describe the door?
C: There is a door that is open. It is daytime. I go through to the outdoors and I am in the country. I notice grass, it is springtime.

Soul Retrieval

Events in our lives frequently take away some power, attribute, or character trait, and we would like to get it back. It is very gratifying to perform a soul retrieval during a past life regression that makes it possible for the client to regain a valuable part of herself. This is referred to as Personality Parts Retrieval in my book *Hypnotherapy: A Client-Centered Approach*.

A client felt she had lost her sense of innocence. Through past life recall, she remembered being sexually assaulted as a young girl by some boys in a neighborhood field. At the end of the regression, my client realized that a part of her soul, a fragment of her personality, had been lost as a result of that event.

During many traumatic events, a part of us is forever altered. Sometimes a desired characteristic has shrunk, or it has been hidden, scattered, taken, or left behind. If you detect that this has happened to your client, you can guide him through a technique known as Soul Retrieval or Personality Parts Retrieval. Through visualization, the client returns to the scene where the event occurred. Now, beginning with a moment when he still had the positive characteristic affected by the trauma, ask him to describe the characteristic metaphorically, giving it a shape and a color. Guide him to move ahead slowly until he notices that he no longer has this characteristic part of himself.

Ask the client to locate this part of himself and retrieve it. While he is holding the part, ask him what he would like to do with it. Most clients say they want to reintegrate it into the body or energy field. Have him do this as best he can. Finally, have him start once again at the beginning of the event. As he moves through it this time, ask him to consciously retain control of the part.

Carrying Wisdom from One Life to the Next

While your client is in a regression, it can be an interesting exercise to strike up a conversation between her and her counterpart in a former life. In this way, she can imagine sharing wisdom and advice with her past life self. Although it is difficult to discern in what ways this activity actually changes any part of the past life, it generally has a profound impact on the present life of the client.

During a regression session, a client saw herself as an atypical woman for her times. She had gone off to the city to learn about people and to write about her experiences. "She never marries. I see her as much older now. She is a strong woman, more of a philanthropist. She spends her time helping people and understanding them, helping people to understand their identity."

When asked what she had learned from having viewed that past life, my client said, "In that past life I accomplished my goals. I have learned that I must keep my creativity and expression open. I understand now that independence is not just about earning income, it is about being true to your dreams. Regardless of the times, I can be true to my dreams if I am creative enough. What I was doing in that life didn't feel like work. I was loving it and loving myself."

Exploring the correlations between that lifetime and the present one, she made this observation: "There are many similarities with my present life. I want to have a center to help people develop their passions and to facilitate their exploration of who they are and what their beliefs are. I have struggled with my identity and my decisions in this life. They were always based on the impressions and opinions of others."

Sharing advice from one life to another

I frequently ask clients if they would like to share their wisdom or observations with their past life counterparts, or if they would like to receive words of wisdom from themselves in a past life. It can be quite enlightening and useful, and it leaves one wondering if those whispers of inspiration that we sometimes receive are perhaps a future life coming back to visit.

A client had come for several sessions to work through stressful issues in her life. We had used several other techniques, making many positive changes, and we decided to complete our third session with a past life regression. The client received a valuable insight from her past life counterpart.

> C: I'm outdoors. It is daytime and I'm in the country. I see trees, a farm, horses, crops, plows, and dirt. I am just observing it.
> ML: What do you notice?
> C: We are working, plowing. There are many of us. I feel old.
> ML: What else do you know about that scene?

C: I'm a woman living on a farm with my large family: a husband and ten children. We all work together on the farm. I was in my 90s when I died.

ML: If you could speak with her, what advice would she give you?

C: Life is simple. You make it harder than it has to be. We worked hard, and we had a lot of love in the family. We gave one another a lot. We worked together to make it, to have food to eat. It was hard work, but it was okay because we all worked together.

ML: What correlations do you see between that lifetime and this one?

C: I need to find people who know how to love. I want to work with people who will work with me. It doesn't have to be so difficult. Many, many people go through life without doing it right. They do someone else's thing, not their own. They follow other people's dreams and miss their own.

ML: What have you learned from this?

C: I need to believe in myself and love myself. The rest will come.

It is powerful to learn to respect your own path and follow your own destiny. So often we are taught that other people come first, and that what others say is more important than our own knowledge. Be true to yourself, then find others who find delight in supporting you. This will make your life happier and more fulfilling.

CHAPTER NINE
Integrating the Work

A female client wants to find out about her career path and her purpose. Her impatience, short temper with people, and frustration at work are starting to bother her. She also wants to learn more about her relationship with Tim, her significant other. She's curious to know why they are together and whether they are soul mates. At the beginning of her visualization session, she's not sure where she is. She describes her location as being in the air, "just observing." The air contains fumes and it is neither light nor dark. She decides to find out more about her surroundings. Taking a step to discover what is behind the thick air, she goes through it and finds herself alone.

    ML: What else do you notice?
    C: There is an opening. I see blue sky and clouds.
    ML: What do you notice about yourself?
    C: I am a male, about 30 years old.
    ML: Do you notice anything else about your surroundings?
    C: I am indoors. It is a closed space, much like a museum. I am looking at statues and art. I walk through the museum, calm and relaxed, observing the sculptures. Then I leave and I'm outside this major museum, at the top of some stairs. I seem to be in Europe, perhaps Italy or London. I come down the stairs into an alley. The streets are beautiful but I don't see many people, in fact, I don't see anyone. This appears now to be a stone city. I wander around with no particular goal. I see a huge rock in front of me, as though the earth has split here. It appears to be an abyss. I am on a cliff and I see waves below, the ocean looks viscous. Now there is a storm, and still no one is around. I jump off the cliff onto the beach and begin to walk along. This appears to be Kauai, with 22 miles of sand and beach. Some local kids push me to hurry so I can see the fire. It is a local ritual with music, many sounds, and a Hawaiian pig roasting. I wait my turn to enjoy the pig meat.

ML: Then what do you do?

C: I am just observing and participating, enjoying myself, relaxed. There is balance and we all seem to be in tune with each other. We know how to enjoy ourselves. I am wearing a black suit, which doesn't fit this event. I want to stay and participate but I have to go back to my village, so I climb up the cliff. I wonder what I should do next, and I fly out of that male body. I just go. I see myself flying up through the clouds, into space. I see the galaxy. It's pretty. I circle around it, enjoying the flight. There is no agenda, no hurry.

ML: Do you notice any correlation between that lifetime and this one?

C: I was carefree there, I had no fear, I could enjoy myself, I was free of obstacles. I was in balance and harmony. I could travel the world, not just be in the office. I was independently wealthy and could help others. It felt good.

ML: Move through the astral experience, up to the time just before you chose to be in this body. What do you notice about that experience?

C: I have confidence. I am not weak but rather strong.

ML: What purpose did you have in choosing to come into this lifetime?

C: I wanted to learn not to worry, to be patient, and to be self-accepting. I wanted to strengthen my ego. To be aware, loving, and kind. To be calm, and to learn to enjoy life.

ML: How will this experience change what you do in the future in this lifetime?

C: I will change careers. I have to come up with an idea for a new business. I will go to a different country. Maybe I will win the lottery or get an inheritance.

ML: Let's continue to explore these issues by asking your subconscious mind to take you to yet another lifetime that will give you even more information. As I count from three to one, you can go to another past life. Three, two, one. Where do you find yourself?

C: I see bright red all around me. The wind is blowing through me.

ML: What else do you notice about that experience?

C: I am wearing a red dress from about the 18th century. I have beautiful red hair.

ML: What do you notice around you?

C: I am in a bar; I am the owner of this bar. It has a joyful atmosphere, we are in good spirits, and I feel the connectedness of everyone. This reminds me of a Western movie because there are horses and carriages.

ML: Some time passes and what do you notice next?

C: I am in a restaurant. We are attacked and there is a looting. Someone tries to kill me with a knife.

ML: What else do you know about that?

C: We are attacked by robbers. All the patrons in the bar die, including me. I have a knife through my stomach.

ML: What else do you know about that?

C: I didn't like it. It was a good life but it was so short.

ML: How do you feel about that lifetime?

C: I was fulfilled.

ML: What have you learned from that lifetime that would be of help to you in this life?

C: I need to start a business that centers around helping people. In that lifetime I was single, and I wished that I had a family. I want to live life to the fullest, to enjoy every minute with no regrets. I have learned that it is important to live life as though I may die tomorrow.

ML: Ask your subconscious to take you to yet another lifetime. Where do you find yourself next?

C: I see black, with fresh paint. It seems to be something new. I am floating comfortably, higher and higher. I am surrounded by cupids and angels, and we all hold hands in a circle. It is like a beautiful painting. One of them looks like my boyfriend, Tim, but with big cheeks. Now it is just the two of us, floating and holding hands. We come to a beautiful castle, like a palace, it might be ice or crystal. I come to the door, open it, and walk in. It is like a cathedral inside; there is a long hallway, perhaps like a large Catholic church. We keep walking. Something jumps out at us and we run to the door. A green light seems to push us onto the central altar. A bad man is floating around, no, a creature that sits and watches. I send healing light to the creature and it goes away, seeming to disintegrate. We run to the door and something stops us, pushing us to the altar once again. We then kiss and get married. An older person does the ceremony.

ML: What do you think this means to you?

C: I see it as meaning we have resolved our differences. We have made peace in front of a spiritual authority who seems very pleased. We rush toward the door, walk out of it, and begin to fly.

ML: What do you experience next?

C: We are dancing and flying. When we come back to Earth we have lost our charm and look like ordinary people. We are in a house, just being people: we dance and bicker and fight over little stuff. The male kills the female, but it is hard to tell who is who—whether I am the male or the female. We are tired and exhausted from the fighting. It is a bad situation, we argue constantly.

ML: What have you learned from experiencing this?

C: This lifetime is better. We have been given a chance in this lifetime to correct the killing from that lifetime. We have the opportunity not to repeat the same mistakes. We can make it work. We are like one person.

ML: What can you do to make it right in this lifetime?

C: I can listen to him, pleasantly and cheerfully, and try to get along. That would feel better. He would be pleasant back, which he is, mostly. I would get more out of him if I were more pleasant.

ML: And now ask the subconscious mind to take you to one last experience, one that will give you helpful information about this. Three, two, one. What do you notice now?

C: I am a man, possibly a soldier or a fire fighter. I am looking for something. There is a fire in front of me, a big one, across a whole field, and I have to put it out alone. It is an enormous job to do alone. I am so tired and I wish I had help. There are more fires on this little planet. I am here to protect the planet.

ML: What do you know about yourself?

C: I am a monstrous, powerful, nonhuman creature. I don't have normal skin; it is more like the thick scales of a snake or lizard. Nothing gets through it. I am here to protect the planet, which is so tiny that I can sit on it and see the rest of the universe. I am all alone.

ML: What else do you notice?

C: The air is thick with fire and smoke. I am lonely and bored, there is no one else around. I fall off the planet, and I am nowhere at all.

ML: What do you notice next?

C: I was powerful, huge, angry, and passionate. I didn't need to eat or drink, nor did I have any feelings. From being about six or eight feet tall I could stretch myself out to be as big as a dinosaur. Still, I had some human features. It seemed I could take on any form and then go back to normal.

ML: What have you learned from that experience?
C: I don't want to be like that anymore. Yet I want to be more flexible in my relationships. It is important to reach out to others.

It is interesting to note that when the session began she was in thick air, and again, at the very end, she experienced thick smoke and fire in the air. It's impossible to know whether she had come full circle or whether it was a different, yet similar, experience.

During about two hours of regression, this client captured memories from four lifetimes, gained a greater understanding of what to do with her present life, and received information that considerably changed her perspective on her relationship.

There are a lot of unanswered questions here. Do you think that her vision of flying with cupids and exchanging vows with her boyfriend was metaphorical? Could it have been an astral experience or a series of memories from between lives? When she flew out of the male body, did she step out of that life and have an astral experience, or did she remember a dream or fantasy? Was the final memory about living on another dimensional plane, or was it metaphorical? It will take further research before she can determine the answers. It is important to note that it is not the function of the regressionist to interpret another person's experiences.

Homework for the Client

This section provides some ideas for homework you can give your clients, which will help support them in understanding and extending their experiences, and in making positive changes in their lives.

Simple recall

Some past lives are discovered spontaneously and may be revealed through casual, off-hand remarks about the possibility of being some person during a particular era. Later, through more formal regression methods, it is possible to confirm whether the client's comments hold any merit. Sometimes the spark of a past life memory is close but not entirely accurate, and sometimes it is right on target. Just as memories concerning activities of five years ago may fade and become distorted, so, too, memories of experiences from 500 years ago may need repeated study to improve accuracy.

While it may take lengthy practice to be able to simply recall past lives accurately, this method is ideal.

Visualizing during meditation

Experiment with various methods that allow your client to enter the state of imagination and discovery, and which will enhance her memory recall. Learn what works best. You might try these methods:

- visualizing going down a hall and choosing a door to enter; this begins a past life regression.
- choosing an era or a location and making up a story about it. At a certain point the details of the story may begin to indicate that one is remembering an actual past life.
- imagining being in a fog. When it lifts, the client discovers himself in a scene from another lifetime.

Encourage your client to give herself permission to have this quiet time, to be open to the experience, and to enjoy the adventure.

Journals

Keeping a journal will help the client extract the details of her regressions. Writing allows us to connect more fully with the events, visions, and emotions of our memories, while at the same time affording the opportunity to clarify our experiences. When we take our time to thoughtfully write out past life explorations, we often discover that we remember even more than we thought we did.

Guided visualization via audiotape

Many prerecorded CDs and tapes are available on the market that can guide you or your client through a past life experience. Some CDs are offered in conjunction with this book, and you'll find ordering information at the back.

Tapes and CDs work well for typical past life memory recall. They are most effective when the client is receptive to the experience and capable of relaxing, visualizing, and receiving the thoughts, visions, feelings, and experiences that such tapes will conjure. Audiotapes function even better if he has experienced at least one regression under the guidance of a live facilitator, who can help him become accustomed to the way he receives and processes this type of information.

You or your clients can make your own audiotapes by recording an induction along with a guided session for attaining a past life. If you would like to do so, you can refer to the script in chapter 3 for ideas. You are welcome to record this guided meditation for your own purposes, but not for sale, as it is copyrighted. When recording, speak slowly and be sure to pause after questions.

Meditation and self-hypnosis

Meditation can reveal many facets of past lives. The use of meditation to remember a past life is similar to the use of self-hypnosis. Both self-hypnosis and meditation can require a certain amount of practice before one achieves success with them. The client must be willing to go into the resulting experience, and must be able to stay focused. Many people also report that they fall asleep before they have completed the regression.

Whether you are using guided visualizations, self-hypnosis, or meditation, the more you practice with past life regression, the more easily you will experience your desired results. Some people say they have difficulty moving through painful memories during self-guided regressions, and some are halted by the same blocks they experience in other areas of their lives. If you are shielding anything from your conscious awareness, it will remain secreted away until you are willing to examine the information fully and to experience the emotions surrounding it.

Dreams

Many people can remember dreams in which they are playing a part from another era. They are in period clothing and they have distinct occupations and relationships with people in that other time. These are often experiences of astral projection during sleep when, traveling through time and space, you discover that you are visiting a previous lifetime.

Because people often astral project spontaneously during dreamtime, dreams are viable ways of visiting alternative lives. Lucid dreams are those that the dreamer directs or controls. To help them experiment with lucid dreaming, you can instruct the client to program her mind with her specific objectives as she is falling asleep, at night or during a daytime nap. The client can direct the dream by programming his mind to visit a particular lifetime about which he is curious. The client can also program her mind to visit a lifetime when she had a relationship with a certain person, when she had a specific occupation, or when she understood a certain body of knowledge.

While concentrating on the objective, you might also encourage the client to program his mind to remember the dream when he wakes up. It often works well to imagine bringing your energy into your forehead, while remaining aware of your experience as you fall asleep. It feels as though your body is sleeping while your mind remains vigilant, observing the process and the experience. Then, as you awaken, stay focused on what you were dreaming. At first you may only remember emotions, feelings, or moods, or you may remember objects, colors, people, or situations. Your client may be among those who can easily remember their dreams, or he may not. With practice, however, most people can learn to do this well.

As with astral projection, dreams involving past lives will have a distinct quality. Because you are aware during the dream, you can manipulate your reactions. Additionally, the experience somehow feels more real or more tangible. Even daydreams may spark memories that can later be confirmed as past lives. Tell your clients to allow their fantasy world to be fertile, to conjure up new possibilities and probabilities. Then follow up their fantasies with diligent research and regressions to sort out fact from fantasy.

Familiar locations

Perhaps your client experiences going somewhere new, and suddenly remembers some odd detail she wasn't aware that she knew. It might be information about the streets of a strange town, knowledge of hidden rooms in a cathedral, or the location of a cave in a mountainside or a cemetery in the country. In cases like these, the subconscious mind recognizes the scene even when the conscious mind doesn't. When your client experiences sensations of familiarity, encourage them to take a moment to relax and allow their imagination to conjure pictures, ideas, and possibilities.

Art

Clients sometimes become aware of a flood of memories or even a hint of déjà vu after viewing artwork or a movie. These experiences can be very distinct signposts of a past life memory. You can experiment with this yourself. The next time you visit an art museum, notice the paintings to which you are drawn. Relax into the experience and observe whether any memories or feelings seem to surface. Do the paintings that attract you depict scenes of a certain era? Do you recognize an activity or a location? Do the paintings elicit emotions and memories that are not apparently related to events in this lifetime?

Aesthetics are our concepts and values made concrete. Perhaps a painting or sculpture elicits emotions, feelings, and memories that, when explored, can produce similar experiences remembered from other lifetimes. Although the artwork may not depict an exact past live event, it may elicit a reaction that is associated with an actual memory.

Childhood games

What were the client's favorite childhood games? Teacher, artist, musician, doctor, or nurse? Fireman, mommy, superhero, or cowboy? Royalty, pirate, spy, dancer, or cook? These preferences can give clear indications of past life experience. Children are innocent and open regarding knowledge of their purpose and past life experiences. They naturally gravitate to roles with which they are comfortable or familiar.

Many parents report that their children tell them stories about locations, events, or occupations that they remember participating in. It is highly possible these stories are a result of past life memories. Encouraging such stories and role-playing in children, as well as in adults, can help them enhance their connections to this knowledge.

Epilogue

You gave your life to become the person you are right now. Was it worth it?

—Richard Bach, author, *One*

This message is for you. Though you are counseling others and guarding their experiences of regression, the experience of past lives is important to your process of self-discovery. Contemplate what your subconscious mind will reveal to you in lives to come, when you regress to this present lifetime. Will your memories be exciting? Will they be depressing or confusing? Will you be proud of your adventures or be filled with remorse or regret?

Remember that your subconscious mind is gathering information continuously throughout the day and night. Every thought, every feeling, and every activity is recorded and saved. What are you doing to ensure that your memories are going to be worthwhile? What are you doing to add depth, growth, expansion, balance, and love of self and life to your soul's experience?

Are you, in fact, paying attention to your life? Do you live in the present moment, or is your mind always wandering into the past or the future? How will you remember this lifetime if you have not spent time focusing on it?

Your soul's quest for self-discovery and enlightenment is the driving force underlying your behaviors, actions, reactions, emotions, and pursuits. It is the most delightful and fascinating journey in which you will ever participate.

Be the hero of your own saga. Meet the challenge. Participate fully in the depths and heights of this physical experience to bring home your own brass ring, your personal holy grail: knowledge of your true self.

Recommended Reading

Adams, Douglas, *Hitchhiker's Guide to the Galaxy* (Random House Value Pub., 1996).

Bach Richard, *One* (Dell Books, Reissued 1989).

Bach, Richard, *Bridge Across Forever* (Dell Books, Reissued 1986).

Binswanger, Harry, Ed., *Ayn Rand Lexicon* (Penguin Books, 1986).

Cunningham, Janet, *A Tribe Returned* (Deep Forest Press, 1994).

Davies, Paul, *God & The New Physics* (Simon & Schuster, 1983).

Davies, Paul, *Mind of God* (Simon & Schuster, 1992).

Fiori, Edith, *The Unquiet Dead* (Ballantine Books, 1991).

Ingram, Julia, and Hardin, G.W., *The Messengers: A True Story of Angelic Presence and the Return to the Age of Miracles* (Pocket Star, 1997).

LaBay, Mary Lee, *Hypnotherapy: A Client-Centered Approach* (Pelican Publishing, 2003).

LaBay, Mary Lee, and Hogan, Kevin, *Through the Open Door: Secrets of Self-Hypnosis* (Pelican Publishing, 2000).

Lucas, Winafred Blake, Ph.D., *Regression Therapy: A Handbook for Professionals Vol. I & II* (Deep Forest Press, Reissued 1999).

Moody, Raymond A., M.D., *Life After Life* (Harper, 2001).

Phillips, Maggie, and Frederick, Claire, *Healing the Divided Self* (W.W. Norton & Co., 1995).

Swartz, Gary E.R., *The Afterlife Experiments* (Pocket Star, 2002).

Talbot, Michael, *Holographic Universe* (HarperCollins, 1991).

Talbot, Michael, *Mysticism and the New Physics* (Penguin Group, Revised 1993).

Watson, Lyall, *Beyond Supernature* (Bantam Books, 1989).

Weiss, Brain L., M.D., *Many Lives Many Masters* (Fireside, 1988).

Index

Analytical Imp	124
Ancestor	90
Anchoring	51
Art	135
Aspects	78, 81, 84
Associated	50, 51
Astral	80, 93, 100, 101, 108, 130, 132
Astral Plane	63, 83, 84, 109, 110
Astral Projection	63, 83, 111, 134
Auditory	64, 65, 66
Behavior	16, 29, 43, 45, 46, 47, 78, 100, 107
Belief	24, 42, 47, 53, 54, 55
Between Lifetimes	35, 43, 99, 100
Between Lives	38, 40, 78, 84, 97, 99, 100, 102, 110, 132
Chaos	27, 28, 37
Childhood Abuse	35
Childhood Games	135
Children	31, 32, 41, 45, 49, 54, 58, 61, 70, 71, 90, 99, 101, 135
Consciousness	24, 28, 75, 78, 80, 81, 83, 84, 95, 99, 100, 101, 105, 106, 108, 109
Creative Visualization	53
Death	42, 43, 61, 69, 70, 71, 79, 83, 90, 95, 99, 100, 101, 107, 109, 110
Decisions	16, 22, 31, 39, 52, 78, 86, 106, 107
Dimensions	80, 82, 83
Dissociated	50, 51, 52
Divorce	34, 104
Dreams	16, 43, 59, 66, 67, 134
Emotional	22, 23, 62, 63, 64, 66, 67, 83, 101, 113
Energy	29, 33, 45, 46, 48, 49, 63, 83, 95, 100, 101, 116, 126, 134
Etheric	83
Eye Movement	60

False Memory 57, 59, 61, 63
Famous 86
Fantasy 60, 61, 132, 135
Fear 27, 34, 42, 43, 45, 69, 74, 91, 104
Filters 54, 55, 57, 62, 63, 64, 66, 100
Future 78, 79, 84
Gender 29, 33, 49
Goals 16, 27, 48, 94, 96, 113
Guided Visualization 53, 133
Habits 16, 24, 86, 95, 96, 107
Headaches 116
Historical Records 61
Hypnotherapy 17, 22, 24, 46, 48, 51, 113, 126
Imagination 47, 48, 49, 53, 54, 57, 81, 83, 132, 135
Induction 48
Infinite 80, 85
Intuition 61, 65
Journal 47, 133
Kinesthetic 64, 65
Languages 34
Lessons 17, 22, 24, 25, 29, 31, 42, 43, 46, 47, 58, 78, 94, 101, 105, 106, 107, 108
Marriage 17, 29, 31, 34, 49
Meditation 47, 85, 132, 133, 134
Mental 83
Metaphor 22, 47, 50, 67, 116, 117
Music 48
My Father 109
Object Imagery 17, 27, 35, 48, 50, 113, 116
Oblivion 35, 39
Outcomes 119, 120, 121
Parenting 38
Parts Therapy 113, 119, 121
Perception 35, 55, 61, 67, 100
Personality 15, 33, 40, 45, 52, 63, 85, 86, 92, 95, 96, 100, 126
Philosophy 24, 54
Phobias 23, 43
Point of Focus 84
Pre-Birth Choices 104
Preternatural 83
Progression 79
Purpose 15, 16, 24, 26, 27, 28, 33, 37, 40, 41, 47, 75, 79, 92, 93,
.... 94, 95, 96, 101, 105, 106, 107, 108, 119, 129, 135
Race 25, 29, 34, 52
Rapport 48, 50
Reality 24, 27, 28, 31, 43, 52, 53, 54, 57, 62, 63, 67, 78, 81, 95, 100
Recognize 29, 33, 39, 102, 109, 135
Reframing 46, 113

Index

Regression Sessions
- Adoption 38
- Analytical Imp 124
- Between Lives 102
- Boredom 16
- Bow and Arrow 66
- Camelot 59
- Childbirth on Beach 99
- Childhood Abuse 35
- Core Values 28
- Daughter Relationship 32
- Decisions 106
- Different Races/Genders 34
- Estranged Father 63
- Favorite Uncle 71
- Flat Relationship 29
- For Love 105
- Gladiator 87
- Gold Rush 29
- Harsh Lessons 95
- Health Challenges 116
- Jazz Musician 25
- Life Purpose 75
- Miner's Death 70
- Multiple Lives 129
- Multiple Sclerosis 21
- My Father 109
- Nazis 43
- Neck Pain 27
- Off Planet 79
- Phobias 23
- Removing Blocks 113
- Rock Musician 93
- Roots of Emotions 71
- Seizure Disorder and Migraines 17
- Serial Killer 46
- Sharing Advice 127
- Sharing Bodies 96
- Stepping in Japan 97
- Stepping Out 94
- Trading Places 92
- Unexplained Pain 22
- Unfaithful Husband 34
- Weight Issues 119
- Writer 26

Relationships 15, 16, 24, 29, 31, 32, 38, 39, 49, 58, 71, 74, 78, 85, 107, 132, 134
Removing Blocks 113
Research 39, 52, 57, 61, 62, 96, 132, 135

Reverse Metaphor 116
Safe Space 48, 49
Scientific Method 52
Script for Regression 49
Secondary Gains 113, 119
Self-hypnosis 133, 134
Sexual Orientation 33
Shame 42, 45, 62
Soul 15, 22, 24, 29, 31, 33, 34, 39, 40, 41, 42, 43, 45, 46, 81, 82, 83, 84, 85, 87, 90,
.... 91, 92, 94, 95, 96, 105, 106, 107, 108, 126, 129, 137
Soul Groups 39
Soul Mate 39, 94, 129
Soul Retrieval 126
Space 24, 78, 81, 82, 94, 134
Spirit 24, 33, 69, 75, 81, 84, 85, 87, 92, 93, 94, 95, 96, 97, 98,
.... 100, 101, 102, 105, 106, 107, 108, 109, 110, 111
Stepping In 91, 92, 93, 95, 96, 97, 98
Stepping Out 91, 93, 94, 95, 97
Subconscious Mind 15, 29, 41, 51, 59, 78, 108, 135, 137
Success 51, 86, 133
Techniques
    Analytical Imp 124
    Anchoring 51
    Associated 50, 51
    Dissociated 50, 51, 52
    Induction 48
    Object Imagery 116
    Outcomes 119
    Parts Therapy 121
    Reframing 46, 113
    Reverse Metaphor 116
    Safe Space 48, 49
    Script for Past Life Regression 49
    Secondary Gains 119
    Soul Retrieval 126
Unexplained Pain 22, 27, 113
United States Geological Survey 80
Values 28, 135
Violence 107
Visual 64, 65, 66, 100, 118
Visualization 29, 35, 53, 75, 116, 124, 126, 129, 133
Walk-in 91

Additional Products from Mary Lee LaBay

Books

Hypnotherapy: A Client-Centered Approach	$24.95
Through the Open Door: Secrets of Self-Hypnosis With Kevin Hogan, Ph.D.	$22.00
Irresistible Attraction: Secrets of Personal Magnetism With Kevin Hogan, Ph.D.	$19.95

Guided Meditation CD's

Each $19.95 or three for the price of two $39.90

(Call for low wholesale prices when purchasing merchandise for resale.)

Explore a Past Life:
Journey through time to learn who you were in previous lifetimes. Discover dates, places, occupation, talents, relationships with others and more.

Discover Your Life Purpose:
Enter the "Do and Be Room" where you will learn what your true soul purpose was meant to be and what you agreed to accomplish in this lifetime.

Your Empowerment Symbol:
A guided meditation to reconnect you to your innate power and confidence. Receive a symbol from your subconscious mind that will anchor this empowered state for future use.

Artistic Creativity:
Connect with your artistic, creative self and immerse yourself in your talents in music, dance, art, or whatever art form you are drawn to. This experience will bring enhanced artistic expression into your present life.

Opening to Prosperity:
Discover what has blocked you from attaining the prosperity that you desire. Open the energy and magnetize that abundance into your life.

Relieve Stress:
Create a Control Panel that allows you to control your blood pressure and stress levels.

Restful Sleep:
Enjoy deep relaxation to sooth away the stress and mind chatter, then embark on a dreamy journey that results in deep restful sleep.

Control Anger:
Understand the underlying hidden causes and remove the specific triggers that lead you to anger.

Remove Road Rage:
Review and analyze your rage experiences, and alter your behavior to new, positive responses.

Smoke No More:
Deep and thorough therapy to remove the secondary gains and root causes of your habit, plus positive behavior modification to ensure your success as a non-smoker.

Effective Weight Loss
  Track A - *Weighty Issues:*
  Explore the deep-seated issues that cause weight gain and retention. Understand the true reasons why your diets and exercise have not worked for you yet.
  Track B - *Weight No Longer:*
  Make deep subconscious changes in your perceptions, thought patterns and emotions so that your body will begin to quickly respond to your diet and exercise programs.

DVD: Healing the Past for Future Health: $89.95 ($97.85 including tax)
Two DVDs - 3 hours of live class – Successful Decision-making, Past Life Regression, Empowerment Symbol, Core Transformation, Healing techniques for anxiety, headaches, hiccoughs, stress and more. Wookbook included.

Books may be ordered through your favorite bookstore or online source.
Books, CDs, and DVDs may be ordered directly from the author.
For a current listing of Events, Courses, Books, CDs, and DVDs please visit:

www.maryleelabay.com

ISBN 1-4120-1278-3

Made in the USA
San Bernardino, CA
26 March 2014